What Happens When We Die?

What Happens When We Die?

What the Scriptures Really Teach

Bill Ledford

What Happens When We Die?
What the Scriptures Really Teach
Copyright ©2017 Bill Ledford

ISBN: 978-1535369619
Religion / Biblical Criticism & Interpretation

Quantity Purchases: Groups may qualify for special terms when ordering quantities of this title. For information: bledford7711@gmail.com.

Printed in the United States of America.
First Edition

Table of Contents

Dedication

Dedicated to all who have the courage to search diligently for truth, the humility to be teachable, the fortitude to weather the storms of change, and the willingness to be hated and persecuted as we are transformed by the renewing of our minds in Christ Jesus.

If the world hate you, ye know that it hated me before it hated you.
(John 15:18)

And be not conformed to this world: but be ye transformed by the renewing of your mind, that ye may prove what is that good, and acceptable, and perfect, will of God. (Romans 12:2)

Introduction

If you knew something I didn't, especially if it could have an adverse effect on my life, I would want you to tell me the truth. My experience has been that's what most people want, too. At the end of the day, we prefer the truth over a lie no matter how painful the betrayal has been. We can at least get on the healing side of the hurt to begin the reconciliation process toward our recovery. It is in this spirit that I offer these treasures for your reflection.

Our battles for truth don't always come easy. It's a fierce war and the casualties will be our favorite fairy tales and delusions, but they will be necessary losses if we desire to know Scriptural truth. We might go through the grieving process to let go of them step by step, one or more steps at the same time, or all the steps at the same time, but we will go through them if we want to overcome.

- Skepticism;
- Ridicule;

- Violently opposed, anger;
- Acceptance as being self-evident.

Finding truth can be simple; accepting the simplicity of truth can be hard.

We often get very upset when someone teaches us what is in the Scriptures rather than what we presume is in the Scriptures. For the seasoned believer, this can be even more disturbing. We may be required to surrender years of cherished but false doctrines in exchange for humble correction and precious truth. I've had to do it many times. It's the sacrifice we all have to make in exchange for the exceedingly great joy and rewards that await us, when we release ourselves from the bondage of lies and live in the freedom of truth.

I have bolded verse text here and throughout for emphasis:

*He that refuseth instruction despiseth his own soul: but **he that heareth reproof getteth understanding.** (Proverbs 15:32)*

Again, the kingdom of heaven is like unto treasure hid in a field; the which when a man hath found, he hideth, and for joy thereof goeth and selleth all that he hath, and buyeth that field. (Matthew 13:44)

*And **ye shall know the truth, and the truth shall make you free.** (John 8:32)*

We can't have fellowship with God if we walk in darkness.

*[5] This then is the message which we have heard of him, and declare unto you, that God is light, and in him is no darkness at all. [6] **If we say that we have fellowship with him, and walk in darkness, we lie, and do not the truth:** (1 John 1:5-6)*

If someone asked you:

- *How did you get here?*
- *Who are you?*
- *Why are you here?*
- *What happens when you die?*

Would you be solid and confident in your answers or would you be like most of the herd at loss for words? When the question is asked: "Do we not know because of ignorance or apathy?" is our response "I don't know, and I don't care."

Our birth and death are the two most significant events in our life, yet they are also the two things we seem to know the least about. It could be our human nature to steer away from the subject of death. Most people will put more time into watching a football game or planning a vacation than searching for the answers to these age-old questions.

These questions became mine long-ago after the death of several loved ones within the same year. Their deaths grabbed my attention! I lacked spiritual understanding back then and was unsure about a Creator. I had been taught there was God and I knew many who believed: also many who did not. I couldn't help but wonder: "What is the truth?" "I want to know, one way or the other for certain." The only sure thing I had going was a deep, inner yearning to know and with God's all-sufficient grace, it would be enough.

I quickly arrived at two more foundational questions that would be essential for my answers.

- *Is there really a God?*
- *If there is God, then what is my relationship with Him supposed to be?*

I took my first step into the unknown by faith and have not regretted my choice, although there were some times I questioned my decision when the going was hard. It hasn't always been easy but it has always been absolutely worth it. I found the answers to my questions. I believe I can help you find the answers to yours.

We are going to answer all the above questions and more. I think you, too, will find value and comfort in knowing theses simple mysteries when you have to face the death of loved ones or your own destined mortality.

But what do *you* want?

If I suggested to you that many of our long-established, traditional beliefs about what happens when we die could be different from the teachings of the Holy Scriptures, would you be interested in knowing what they are? Would you be up for the challenge of testing what you think you know with what God has said and provided for our understanding? Testing our beliefs can be exciting because it is how we learn and grow and become wiser. Imagine where you might be today if you never challenged your beliefs about Santa Claus, the Easter Bunny or the Tooth Fairy. I intend no offense to those who still want to believe.

The key questions to begin discovery are: "Do you want to know?" and "Are you teachable?" The fact that you are reading this book says you probably would answer "yes." Are you willing to uncover self-deception, do you want a fuller revelation, see value in self-examination, and feel passionate about uncovering hidden mysteries and truths? If you are, then you have come to the right place. We are going to closely examine "what the Scriptures really teach" about death.

Notice that I didn't say you will be required to change your beliefs. I am only asking that you be willing to check them at the door for the short time we have together to explore. You can always pick them up again on your way out if you choose. God does not force His will against ours, and this book is not intended to do so either.

"You may choose to look the other way but you can never say again that you did not know."

William Wilberforce (1759-1833)
– Leader of the movement to abolish the slave trade

What to expect – "Just the facts, ma'am."

This book is intended to be brief, to the point, and an easy to follow reference manual; to present the simple facts about what the Holy Scriptures teach about our creation, death, resurrection, future, and the hope that we have in Christ Jesus. It also serves as a call for us to examine what we think we know because we are only seeing a glimpse of the bigger picture for now. Knowing in part means that none of us have all the answers. If we want to expand our horizons of knowledge and understanding, it can be highly advantageous for us to fellowship with other believers who have their part to the puzzle.

*And if any man think that **he knoweth any thing, he knoweth nothing yet as he ought to know.** (1 Corinthians 8:2)*

*[9] **For we know in part,** and we prophesy in part. [10] But when that which is perfect is come, then that which is in part shall be done away. (I Corinthians 13:9-10)*

I have drawn from the Scriptures and arranged them in a discernable order for your understanding. Our plan is to move quickly but without leaving anyone behind. We are going to examine the Holy Scriptures in context and harmony, and let the evidence speak for itself. The goal is that you will be able to make better-informed choices for your life.

Some preparation will be needed.

As with any new adventure, we need to begin first with some preparation. We will also need to reach agreement on some things. The first few chapters will cover both of these before we begin the drill-down process to uncover our answers. It is not difficult, but it will require our attention.

For the most part, we will be using the *King James Version* of the Bible and *Strong's Exhaustive Concordance.* Definitions found listed after verses include the English word chosen by the King James translators followed by Strong's reference number: either the Hebrew (Old Testament) or Greek (New Testament) word used and then a condensed or expanded definition.

Our study about death doesn't profess to list all of the many Scripural references available to us. I have left out many references on purpose because they only tend to repeat what has already been included. I have intentionally kept text concise and simple with few words for fast and easy reading. This book is not intended to be either exhaustive or scholarly.

To accurately discern what the Scriptures say about death, we can't avoid addressing some of the many false doctrines that have influenced our beliefs. As enticing as it is to *rabbit-trail* down as many as we can, we will stay on point and only inspect a few of the major ones that have twisted the truth of God into a lie.

God hasn't made it complicated.

I once heard: *"It's hard to mess up the simplicity of the Bible (Scriptures) unless we've had help, and we've had a lot of help."* (Curry Blake, John G. Lake Ministries International)

God has not complicated things for us. He desires that we intimately know Him, His nature and character. He has given us the truth for our comfort and understanding. As our relationship with Him grows, we begin to see and appreciate the simplicity of His ways.

*But I fear, lest by any means, as the serpent beguiled Eve through his subtilty, so **your minds should be corrupted from the simplicity that is in Christ.** (2 Corinthians 11:3)*

Are you ready?

If you are, then let's get started.

Come to the edge he said.
We are afraid they said.
Come to the edge he said.
We will fall they said.
Come to the edge he said.
They came.
He pushed them.
And they flew.

- Guillaume Apollinaire (1880-1918) - Poet

~ ONE ~

"What we know for sure that just ain't so."

If we attend a funeral and listen closely to what the living say, we quickly discover that there are as many differing opinions about what happens when we die as there are people at the funeral. Everyone seems to have a different thought or opinion about death, even if that thought or opinion is simply not having a clue.

Some of our most commonly held beliefs about death are:

- At the time of death, we either ascend to a glorious heaven or descend to a fiery hell;
- Our bodies die, but our soul or spirit (*consciousness*) remains alive and goes to be with God in heaven. Some also believe the deceased can look down on us and even help direct our lives;
- Death is the final and permanent end of everything for the deceased;
- We go to a holding place called purgatory;

- We go to some other place: Paradise, Shambhala, Nirvana, Elysium, Valhalla, etc.;
- We reincarnate for another life;
- And the long list continues ...

"Purgatory: a state after death according to Roman Catholic belief in which the souls of people who die are made pure through suffering before going to heaven."

"Reincarnation: the idea or belief that people are born again with a different body after death."

Do we enter the spirit world and become angels or ghosts? Can we be reincarnated and come back again for another life as a human, animal or something else? Can the living communicate with the dead? Can the dead haunt us or the places where they once lived?

Fittingly, our sense of reason tells us that not all of these things can be right. We are often left in confusion as we attempt to sort out the answers. Because Scripture says God is not the author of confusion, then we can know there is something else at work creating the chaos; namely the enemy, "the father of lies."

For God is not the author of confusion, but of peace, as in all churches of the saints. (1 Corinthians 14:33)

Ye are of your father the devil, and the lusts of your father ye will do. He was a murderer from the beginning, and abode not in the truth, because there is no truth in him. When he speaketh a lie, he speaketh of his own: for he is a liar, and the father of it. (John 8:44)

None of these beliefs are accurate.

Most people are usually surprised to learn that according to Scripture, none of these things happen when we die; that's right, NONE! They are all fables *(fictitious tales)* when compared with the clear word and true light of Scripture.

> *[3] For the **time will come when they will not endure sound doctrine;** but after their own lusts shall they heap **to themselves teachers, having itching ears; [4] And they shall turn away their ears from the truth, and shall be turned unto fables.** (2 Timothy 4:3-4)*

When we take God out of our knowledge, common sense and awareness of direction always go with it. Without God as our compass, our fate is to search aimlessly and invent fables for our answers about life and death. Scripture will dispel every myth to reveal:

- Man is formed from the dust of the earth and becomes a *living soul* with the breath of life from God;
- Fallen man is *mortal*;
- Fallen man does not have an *immortal soul*;
- Death is a painless, unconscious sleep with no awareness of time;
- It is not possible to communicate with the dead;
- Jesus Christ died, was buried and raised to life again from the dead;
- Jesus Christ will return and resurrect those who belong to Him, *at His coming*;
- Others will be resurrected at some time to stand before God for judgment;
- There isn't a single verse found in Scripture that says we ascend to a glorious heaven or descend to a fiery hell when we die;

21

- There isn't a single verse found in Scripture that says hell is a place of eternal, fiery torment;
- There isn't a single verse found in Scripture that says we go to heaven, _ever_.

By now have you started to wonder, if all of these things are so, how did we manage to get the train so far from the track? How did we get _from there_ (the teachings of Scripture) _to here_ (the popular but erroneous beliefs being taught today)? Do you think we could we have been deceived along the way, maybe even just a little?

Before we begin to uncover and unravel the lies from the truth, we'll look to see if Scripture has anything to offer us about deception.

That just ain't so.

We can all probably agree that neither Mark Twain (1835-1910) nor Will Rogers (1879-1935) wrote any of the words found in the Holy Scriptures. However, they both have been credited with this slightly paraphrased quote that rightly fits our search for answers:

> _"It ain't what you don't know that gets you into trouble._
> **_It's what you know for sure that just ain't so."_**

This book is your written invitation to walk with me, as we journey to explore the written word of Scripture to discover about death, _"… what we know for sure, **that just ain't so."**_

~ TWO ~

We must be keenly aware of deceptions

Since the time of Christ, over two-thousand years ago, we have lived in a time of great deception and Scripture expressly warns us of this fact. We don't have to be fearful of being deceived, but we do have to realize that deceptions have infected everything we think we know today. They can have a detrimental effect on our lives and well-being. Scripture will teach us how to recognize and avoid them.

We have to learn to be good "Bereans."

When Paul and Silas were teaching the good news of the gospel in Berea, the people listened to their teachings with open minds and then searched the Scriptures daily to confirm the authenticity of their teachings. The reader is likewise strongly encouraged to seek discernment and understanding, to be a good *"Berean"* and receive the word with all readiness (*willingness*) of mind and then search (*examine*) the Scriptures, confirming these things are so.

[10] And the brethren immediately sent away Paul and Silas by night unto Berea ... [11] These were more noble than those in Thessalonica, in that they received the word with all readiness of mind, and searched the scriptures daily, whether those things were so. [12] Therefore many of them believed ... (Acts 17:10-12)

Jesus warned us about deceptions with His Sermon on the Mount of Olives.

Eyewitness accounts are found in the chapters of Matthew 24, Mark 13 and Luke 21. The Sermon on the Mount of Olives is often called the "Olivet Discourse."

Imagine for a moment: we are on the Mount of Olives in the presence of the prophesied Messiah when a few of His disciples approach Him to ask, *"... what shall be the sign of thy coming, and of the end of the world [age]?"* (Matthew 24:3)

We focus our undivided attention on every word as He begins to speak:

*[4] **Take heed that no man deceive you.** [5] For many shall come in my name, saying, I am Christ; and **shall deceive many.** [11] And **many false prophets shall rise, and shall deceive many.** (Matthew 24:4-5, 11)*

The King of kings and Lord of lords just issued a "red-flag-warning" about a barrage of deceptions on a collision course with mankind, with many being deceived before the destruction of Jerusalem and the temple in AD 70. Why do we imagine that there will be any less deception in our day? Unrepentant man's nature has not changed.

Through the gospel writings of Matthew, Mark, and Luke, we can relive this momentous event, but have we heeded His early warning by diligently seeking for Scriptural truth? Have we been conformed to the world by those who would change the truth of God into a lie, or are we being transformed by the renewing of our minds to prove the good, acceptable, and perfect will of God?

And be not conformed to this world: but be ye transformed by the renewing of your mind, that ye may prove what is that good, and acceptable, and perfect, will of God. (Romans 12:2)

Scripture warns us repeatedly.

Scripture has devoted lots of space to alert us about false Christs, prophets, apostles, spirits, and deceitful workers. To ignore these warnings can lead to our peril so we must test every spirit and doctrine we believe by the word of Scripture.

*For there shall arise **false Christs, and false prophets, and shall shew great signs and wonders; insomuch that, if it were possible, they shall deceive the very elect.** (Matthew 24:24)*

*[13] For such are **false apostles, deceitful workers,** transforming themselves **into the apostles of Christ.** [14] And no marvel; for **Satan himself is transformed into an angel of light.** (2 Corinthians 11:13-14)*

*Beloved, **believe not every spirit, but try [test] the spirits whether they are of God:** because many false prophets are gone out into the world. (1 John 4:1)*

*[1] Now the Spirit speaketh expressly, that in the latter times **some shall depart from the faith, giving heed to seducing spirits, and doctrines of devils; [2] Speaking lies in hypocrisy; having their conscience seared with a hot iron;** (1 Timothy 4:1-2)*

*And the great dragon was cast out, that old serpent, called the Devil, and Satan, **which deceiveth the whole world:** he was cast out into the earth, and his angels were cast out with him. (Revelation 12:9)*

We must remember that *"Satan deceives the whole world"* so this includes both you and me. Therefore, we can expect almost all of the people to be wrong about almost everything almost all of the time. What happens at death is no exception, but we have the promise that every hidden lie will come to the light.

All deceptions will be exposed.

Jesus promised that the truth will uncover all deceptions. Man seriously and very wrongly believes that all his secrets, lies, acts, and deeds are going to stay hidden in the darkness. This belief is far from what Scripture teaches. They are all going to be exposed, and man will reap the consequences of his actions.

*For nothing is secret, that shall not be made manifest; **neither any thing hid, that shall not be known** and come abroad. (Luke 8:17)*

*[2] For **there is nothing covered, that shall not be revealed; neither hid, that shall not be known.** [3] Therefore whatsoever ye have spoken in darkness shall be heard in the light; and that which ye have spoken in the ear in closets shall be proclaimed upon the housetops. (Luke 12:2-3)*

*Be not deceived; God is not mocked: **for whatsoever a man soweth, that shall he also reap.** (Galatians 6:7)*

Truth brings freedom: lies bring bondage.

Do we seek Scriptural truth?

We have been warned about deceptions but are we doing anything to learn what they are?

In our prayers, do we humbly ask to be shown where we are being deceived, or do we allow our rebellion and pride to deceive us even deeper by softly whispering in our ear: "*Well, others might be deceived, but not me; I am much too clever for that.*" Do we think we already know the truth and therefore have we closed our hearts to anything that doesn't fit our favorite, cherished doctrines?

How can we know if we have become victims of the lies and deceptions of false prophets and teachers? Are we willing to compare our beliefs to the plain truth of Scripture and allow the Spirit to teach us all things that God freely gives to us?

> *But the Comforter, which is **the Holy Ghost,** whom the Father will send in my name, he shall **teach you all things,** and bring all things to your remembrance, whatsoever I have said unto you. (John 14:26)*

> ***Now we have received, not the spirit of the world, but the spirit which is of God;** that **we might know** the things that are **freely given to us** of God. (1 Corinthians 2:12)*

Are false teachers primarily to blame for our errors if we haven't searched and studied the Scriptures so we can rightly divide (*correctly understand*) the word of truth? Have we sought for discernment and understanding, or have we just accepted every word of false teachers because of their popularity, credentials, education, status, or authority? In the deepest, darkest recesses of our hearts, do we secretly love to believe the lies of false prophesies?

Study to shew thyself approved unto God, a workman that needeth not to be ashamed, *rightly dividing the word of truth.* (2 Timothy 2:15)

The simple [silly, foolish] **believeth every word:** but the prudent man looketh well to his going. (Proverbs 14:15)

The prophets prophesy falsely, and the priests bear rule by their means; and **my people love to have it so:** and what will ye do in the end thereof? (Jeremiah 5:31)

We will see that one popular false prophecy is that we immediately go to heaven when we die instead of going to the grave as Scripture declares. Will we believe the written word of Scripture about this doctrine, or will we believe the lie of the false prophet who offers us a more alluring and enticing way?

False prophets and teachers.

False prophets and teachers have unquestionably influenced our beliefs, but have they done so because of their ignorance or have they done so on purpose? "Ignorance" can come by parroting (*repeating mindlessly*) false teachings and simply passing error on to the next ear. "On purpose" can result from a desire for financial gain, fame, position, lust, and other selfish motives.

Only God can know the secrets of our hearts, but Scripture says that we can know the prophets and teachers by their fruits (*results*). The test is simple. Do their teachings line up and agree with Scripture? If they don't, then they are probably false.

Shall not God search this out? for **he knoweth the secrets of the heart.** (Psalms 44:21)

Wherefore **by their fruits ye shall know them.** *(Matthew 7:20)*

Ultimately, our real enemies are not the false prophets or teachers; they are only puppets in the show. They are being used to distract us from the truth. Our actual adversaries are the evil and wicked influences in the spirit realm. They are manifesting and expressing in the lives of those promoting deception and false doctrines. The enemy has a hierarchy or chain of command with principalities, powers, rulers of darkness, and spiritual wickedness in high places.

For **we wrestle not against flesh and blood,** *but against principalities, against powers, against the rulers of the darkness of this world, against spiritual wickedness in high places. (Ephesians 6:12)*

The false doctrine pile.

Another major problem we all face can be likened to the childhood game of *"Pick-Up Sticks."* A handful of sticks is dropped on a table or floor to form a pile of disarrayed and intertwined sticks, something akin to a mini-log-jam. Game participants take turns to score points by removing sticks from the pile without interrupting or moving another supporting stick.

Have false doctrines dropped upon us in much the same way? As we learn and can carefully remove one false doctrine after another from the pile, there still remain many additional false doctrines – that continue to support the other false doctrines. We have all been victims of it and the only way to win this "false doctrine game" is to let the Spirit teach us how to eliminate the pile completely and to quit playing the game.

A "pile" can also be used to describe something we pick up after our dog. False doctrines should be treated with the same regard and disposed of in like manner. Learn and hold fast to the truth, discard the lies.

Half-truths are lies.

Deceptions can also be the result of "*half-truths,*" where we have received only a portion of the complete story. A half-truth is still a lie. We can also make our own mental jumps and inferences that simply aren't backed up by the written word of Scripture.

Almost everyone has heard the Bible story of the Ark and the great flood. The question:

> "*How many animals of each kind, the male and female,*
> *did God command Moses to take on the Ark?*"

Before reading any further, stop for a few moments to ponder your answer. Then ask yourself:

> "*How old was I when I first heard and learned my answer?*

When you have formulated your answers, please continue reading.

The astute student of Scripture immediately detected that it was Noah and not Moses who built the Ark. Now that we have refocused our attention, simply rephrase the question with, "*How many animals of each kind, the male and female, did God command Noah to take on the Ark?*" Again, decide your answer before you continue reading.

Did you say two? Congratulations! You are in agreement with over 99% of the world with your answer. However, you are only partially correct, and a victim of a lie called a "*half-truth.*" But why shouldn't you be? There have been countless pictures, poems, songs and movies that specifically drilled the answer of two into our minds; but it's only a portion of the whole story.

> *[1] And the LORD said unto Noah, Come thou and all thy house into the ark; for thee have I seen righteous before me in this generation.*

*[2] **Of** every <u>clean beast</u> **thou shalt take to thee <u>by sevens,</u>** the male and his female: and of **beasts that are <u>not clean by two</u>**, the male and his female. (Genesis 7:1-2)*

You are encouraged to conduct your own survey by asking other people this same, simple question. Past surveys have shown that people answer this question correctly less than one-half of one percent of the time. The age when we first learned and believed our answer is usually between five and seven years old.

The question for the diligent searcher for truth now becomes:

> *"If I have been wrong about Scripture for this popularly known belief for most of my life, then how many other things could I be wrong about?"*

Will we now go forth with our newly discovered knowledge or will we despise Scripture because it doesn't fit our current beliefs? Will we plant our feet and hold fast to defend the popular answer of two? The decision is rightly called "our choice."

> *The fear [reverence] of the LORD is the beginning of knowledge: but* **fools despise wisdom and instruction.** *(Proverbs 1:7)*

> *They know not, **neither will they understand; they walk on in darkness:*** *all the foundations of the earth are out of course. (Psalms 82:5)*

We are now aware there can be pitfalls of deceptions and how we can recognize and avoid them. We are ready to move to the next step of our learning, reaching agreement so we can get on the same page together.

Summary.

- We want to learn to be good *Bereans*;
- Jesus repeatedly warned us to be not deceived;
- We are not to be conformed to this world but transformed by the renewing of our minds;
- Scripture repeatedly cautions us that we can and will be deceived;
- All deceptions are going to be exposed;
- We will reap the consequences of our actions;
- We are to seek Scriptural truth;
- The Spirit will teach us all things freely given to us of God;
- There will be false prophets and false teachers;
- False doctrines serve to support other false doctrines;
- A half-truth is a lie;
- Perhaps we don't know everything as we ought to know.

~ THREE ~

Where are the answers?

We learned that we can be deceived. This will be important to remember as we search for the answers to our questions:

- *How did I get here?*
- *Who am I?*
- *Why am I here?*
- *What happens when I die?*
- *Is there really God?*
- *If there is God, then what is my relationship with Him supposed to be?*

Let's examine our last two questions first: "Is there really God?" and "If there is God, then what is my relationship with Him supposed to be?"

Is there really God?

The Scriptures are God's written word _to_ us. Jesus Christ is God's living Word _for_ us. But what if we are unsure there _is_ God?

Scripture affirms that God reveals Himself to all men, so there is no excuse for denying that He exists. The heavens declare His glory, and the firmament (_expanse_) shows His handiwork for all the people to see. This Scriptural text would also mean there is no such thing as an atheist or agnostic, but rather men who want to deny there is God so they can walk in their own way. This rebellious attitude toward God isn't anything new, and we will later learn about the _"BIG LIE"_ to see how the rebellion began and how it continues to plague us today.

> _For the **invisible things of him from the creation of the world are clearly seen, being understood** by the things that are made [men], even his eternal power and Godhead; so that **they are without excuse:** (Romans 1:20)_

> _... The **heavens declare the glory of God;** and the firmament sheweth his handywork. (Psalms 19:1)_

> _The heavens declare his righteousness, and **all the people see his glory.** (Psalms 97:6)_

So, from Scripture we can see:

• _There is God, and we're not Him._

> _Remember the former things of old: for **I am God, and there is none else; I am God, and there is none like me,** (Isaiah 46:9)_

Some may claim this is circular reasoning and doesn't prove God. If you believe this way, then I invite you to go outside on a clear night and ponder the majesty of the night sky, or gaze under a microscope and marvel at the intricacies of creation, so tiny they are invisible to normal sight. None of it happened by random chance.

What is my relationship with Him supposed to be?

This question took me a lot longer to understand. As I continued to search the Scriptures, it finally became clear to me.

* *God is a lot bigger than I first imagined Him to be. I may never fully understand the depths of His nature and character, but I will have forever to discover them. I'm good with that.*

The simple answer is that our individual relationship with our Creator might be very different for each of us, not unlike children in a family where each child contributes his/her special uniqueness. The promise for our future appears to be one of unbelievable amazement and astonishing discovery as we learn and grow in our personal relationship with Him.

> *But as it is written,* **Eye hath not seen, nor ear heard, neither have entered into the heart of man, the things which God hath prepared for them that love him.** *(1 Corinthians 2:9)*

We now know that Scripture proclaims there *is* God. This knowledge is important to establish before we can trust the answers to our other questions. We will also need to reach agreement about some other things before we continue.

Agreement is needed before we move further.

We will cover in detail the agreement we need to reach about:

- Where to search for our spiritual answers;
- That Scripture isn't just read but revealed to us by the Spirit;
- That God moved holy men to write His words of Scripture;
- How we will use Scripture;
- That Scripture must be in harmony, context, and witnessed with other Scripture;
- That men and translations are fallible;
- That what IS NOT WRITTEN can often be just as important as what IS WRITTEN;
- That we will open our self to receive by being teachable, be willing to uncover self-deception, want a fuller revelation, value self-examination, and be passionate for uncovering hidden mysteries and truths;
- Meanings for certain terms we will use.

Can two walk together, ***except they be agreed?*** *(Amos 3:3)*

Where will we search?

Where will we acquire our spiritual information and what source and authority will we use for our answers? Common sense tells us to look to our Creator, the giver of all life, who has provided His written word and Spirit for our understanding. Scripture has many invitations and promises that our answers await us, but we have to take the first step and search for them like hidden treasures.

*[2] So that thou incline thine ear unto wisdom, and apply thine heart to understanding; [3] Yea, if thou criest after knowledge, and liftest up thy voice for understanding; [4] If thou seekest her as silver, and **searchest for***

her as for hid treasures; [5] Then shalt thou understand the fear of the LORD, **and find the knowledge of God.** *(Proverbs 2:2-5)*

We again receive caution that we can't learn something new if we insist we already know the answer. We must humble ourselves and be willing to set aside anything and everything we think we know, so God can teach us what He wants us to know. Learning this is a discipline, which means it can take some practice on our part to truly set-aside our beliefs and learn to become open to new revelation. Seasoned believers need to pay particularly close attention to this. We can easily fall into the trap of thinking we already know, that which we don't know.

Call unto me, *and I will answer thee, and* **shew thee great and mighty things, which thou knowest not.** *(Jeremiah 33:3)*

[12] Then **shall ye call upon me,** *and ye shall go and pray unto me, and* **I will hearken unto you.** *[13] And ye shall* **seek me, and find me,** *when ye shall* **search for me with all your heart.** *(Jeremiah 29:12-13)*

[7] **Ask, and it shall be given you; seek, and ye shall find; knock, and it shall be opened unto you:** *[8] For every one that asketh receiveth; and* **he that seeketh findeth;** *and to him that knocketh it shall be opened. (Matthew 7:7-8)*

The more openly, sincerely, earnestly, humbly, and reverently we seek for the answers, the more likely we are to hear them.

… **The effectual fervent prayer** *of a righteous* **man availeth much.** *(James 5:16)*

The simple truth of the matter is that we will either trust the Scriptures word or we won't. There really isn't any *"in-between-ground"* upon which to stand and we can't have it both ways. If we don't trust them, our beliefs are likely to be tossed to and fro like an un-anchored boat on stormy waves. If we do trust and ground ourselves in them, God is faithful to open His treasures of knowledge, wisdom and understanding, and to awaken us with spiritual discernment.

> *Sanctify [purify] them through thy truth:* **thy word is truth.** *(John 17:17)*

> *Whoever gives heed to instruction prospers, and* **blessed is the one who trusts in the LORD.** *(Proverbs 16:20-New International Version)*

> *[5] Trust in the LORD with all thine heart; and lean not unto thine own understanding. [6] In all thy ways acknowledge him, and* **he shall direct thy paths.** *(Proverbs 3:5-6)*

How will we receive this new information?

Scripture isn't just read but is revealed to us.

When we read the Scriptures, we must realize that Scripture isn't just read for our answers but is "revealed" to us by the Spirit. With this revelation from the Spirit, the words come alive for our discernment and understanding. We could read Scripture a thousand times and still not understand the message, but with revelation and discernment from the Spirit, the message can be revealed to us as quickly as a light switched on to brighten a dark room.

We don't figure it out by our human intellect and reasoning, even if sometimes it feels like we do. God might speak to each of us differently so I am only speaking from my experience.

I learned there is a difference from hearing the Spirit and hearing my thoughts. My thoughts, the Spirit and evil spirits all sounded the same internally so I had to learn how to differentiate between them. The stronger I grew in my knowledge of Scripture, the easier it became for me to discern the voices. Just because something is supernatural doesn't always mean it came from God. I had to learn how to "try" (*test*) the spirits whether they were from God or some other source. Remember the *Bereans* from earlier? They studied the authentic Scriptures daily so they could easier recognize a counterfeit when they saw it.

> *Beloved,* **believe not every spirit, but try** [test] **the spirits** *whether they are of God: because many false prophets are gone out into the world. (1 John 4:1)*

Man's reasoning is fallible which means he can make mistakes. False doctrines derive from man's vain attempts to determine right and wrong in his own eyes, instead of hearing from God. Formal education is not a replacement for hearing the Spirit and will not deliver us from errors. We will see examples of this a little later.

Scripture says that only those "of God" can hear His words, those "not of God" cannot hear His words. Because the "natural man" is not of God, he cannot hear God's words. Spiritual words only sound absurd and foolish to him. If we want to hear from God, we must "*get God*" and to do that, we must first "*get Jesus Christ.*" If you don't yet know them, maybe it's now time for you to meet them.

> *[12]* **Now we have received, not the spirit of the world, but the spirit which is of God;** *that we might know the things that are freely given to us of God. [13] Which things also we speak,* **not in the words which man's wisdom teacheth, but which the Holy Ghost teacheth;** *comparing spiritual things with spiritual. [14] But* **the natural man receiveth not the things of the Spirit of God: for they are foolishness unto him: neither can he know them, because they are spiritually discerned.** *(1 Corinthians 2:12-14)*

*He that is **of God heareth** God's words: **ye** therefore **hear them not, because ye** are **not of God**. (John 8:47)*

Whosoever denieth the Son, the same hath not the Father: *(but) he that acknowledgeth the Son hath the Father also. (1 John 2:23)*

Did God write Scripture or did man?

When holy men first wrote down the words found in Scripture, they were "*in the spirit*" and did not write their thoughts or ideas. Instead, they were moved by God's Spirit to speak and write what He inspired (from "*in*" and "*spirit*") them to write.

No prophecy of Scripture is left to man's private interpretation. Scripture will interpret itself within other verses found in the Old and New Testaments, but these verses must follow the rules of context, harmony (*agreement*), and witness.

*[20] Knowing this first, that **<u>no prophecy of the scripture is of any private interpretation</u>**. [21] **For the prophecy came not** in old time **by the will of man: but holy men of God spake as they were moved by the Holy Ghost**. (2 Peter 1:20-21)*

*[16] **All scripture is given by inspiration of God, and is profitable** for doctrine, for reproof, for correction, for instruction in righteousness: [17] That the man of God may be perfect, thoroughly furnished unto all good works. (2 Timothy 3:16-17)*

The Lord gave the word: *great was the company of those that published it. (Psalms 68:11)*

How should we use Scripture?

If we honestly want to uncover Scriptural truth, we can't "*cherry pick*" single verses or parts of verses to form our favorite doctrines. Verses must be viewed in context, harmonize (*agree*), and be witnessed by other verses.

Simply, we can't select a single verse upon which to base a doctrine when it contradicts a dozen other verses on the same subject. "*A single verse does not necessarily a doctrine make.*" Doing so seems to be one of the biggest mistakes we all make when studying Scripture. The solution is to use simple rules: 1) seek for understanding; 2) find other related verses for the subject under study; 3) read them all in context with several verses before and after; 4) compare them all for agreement and; 5) note where Scripture witnessed them more than once.

Throughout Scripture we find that two or three witnesses establish matters. Therefore, we can expect to find at least two, three, or more supporting passages as witnesses for any doctrine. If we can't find them or somebody can't show them to us, then we are to be suspicious of the doctrine. My preference is to locate agreement in both the Old and New Testaments for continuity and accuracy.

> *One witness shall not rise up against a man for any iniquity, or for any sin, in any sin that he sinneth:* **at the mouth of two witnesses, or at the mouth of three witnesses, shall the matter be established.** *(Deuteronomy 19:15)*

> *But if he will not hear thee, then take with thee one or two more, that* **in the mouth of two or three witnesses every word may be established.** *(Matthew 18:16)*

> *Against an elder receive not an accusation, but* **before two or three witnesses.** *(1 Timothy 5:19)*

Men and translations are fallible.

After we have found our supporting verses from Scripture, we need to be aware of mistakes that come from men and translations.

Some believe the *King James Version* of the Bible is the inspired, infallible, and inerrant word of God to men in the English language. They often believe that all other translations are corrupt and that you should avoid them.

Most are unaware that in the original *1611 King James Version* of the Bible, there is a lengthy preface entitled "*The Translators to the Reader.*" The translators explained that they sought to do a better translation but cautioned us that their work fell short of the original handed down from God. They also encouraged us to search a variety of translations for even deeper understanding of the Scriptures:

"… the original thereof being from heaven, not from earth; the author being God, not man; the inditer [editor], the Holy Spirit, not the wit of the Apostles or Prophets …"

"Truly (good Christian Reader) we never thought from the beginning, that we should need to make a new Translation, nor yet to make of a bad one a good one … but to make a good one better, or out of many good ones, one principal good one …"

"… that variety of Translations is profitable for the finding out of the sense of the Scriptures …"

Man is fallible (*capable of making mistakes*) so every version and translation will have errors. The *King James Version* is no exception as we will later see. Not to worry though, we have God's Holy Spirit to teach and guide us around any errors.

Where there was controversy or the translators were unsure about the clarity of text, they added margin notes so the reader could seek further. These notes were to keep the reader from concluding they were reading incontrovertible truth not subject to further debate or dispute. One source counts 8,422 margin notes in the original version and the translators argued strongly for their inclusion.

> "**Some** peradventure [perhaps] **would have no variety of senses to be set in the margin,** lest the authority of the Scriptures for deciding of controversies by that show of uncertainty should somewhat be shaken. But **we hold their judgment not to be so sound in this point** ... It hath pleased God in his Divine Providence here and there to scatter words and sentences of that difficulty and doubtfulness, not in doctrinal points that concern salvation (for in such it hath been vouched that the Scriptures are plain), but in matters of less moment, that **fearfulness would better beseem us than confidence** ... Now in such a case **doth not a margin do well to admonish the Reader to seek further, and not to conclude or dogmatize** [represent as incontrovertible truth] **upon this or that peremptorily** [subject to no further debate or dispute]? ... that **variety of translations is profitable for finding out of the sense of the Scriptures:** so diversity of signification and sense in the margin, where the text is not so clear, must needs do good; **yea, is necessary, as we are persuaded ... They that are wise had rather have their judgments at liberty in difference of readings, than to be captivated to one, when it may be the other.**" (The Translators to the Reader, *1611 King James Version* of the Bible)

Italicized words found in the *King James Bible* are words not found in the available manuscripts at the time of translation. Translators added these words in an attempt to help the reader's understanding. These additional words are often very helpful but sometimes can alter the meanings of the thoughts being expressed and be detrimental to our comprehension. Therefore, it is suggested to read passages both ways, with and without these "*italicized words*" and then compare the message with other Scripture in context, precept upon precept, and line upon line.

[9] Whom shall he teach knowledge? and whom shall he make to understand doctrine? them that are weaned from the milk, and drawn from the breasts. [10] **For precept must be upon precept, precept upon precept; line upon line, line upon line; here a little, and there a little:** *(Isaiah 28:9-10)*

> Precept: H6673, *tsav*: an injunction [authoritative order], a command, commandment.
> Line: H6957, *qav*: a cord (as connecting), especially for measuring.

There are those who will argue that God would not give us corrupted Scripture. We must remember that God didn't give us corrupted Scripture, man did. But why would God allow man to corrupt His word? Consider that one reason might be to draw us into a closer relationship with Him. It requires us to learn how to hear and communicate "one-on-one" with Him in the spirit. Man's way in the past was to have a prophet or priest hear for him from God.

What *IS NOT WRITTEN* can be as important as what *IS WRITTEN.*

The silence of things "not written" in Scripture can often convey as much significance for our understanding as things that "are written." In the fast paced, noisy world of today, our hearing can become dulled to the whisper of silence found within the words. We must learn to tune our hearing to the still small voice of the LORD.

[11] And he said, Go forth, and stand upon the mount before the LORD. And, behold, the LORD passed by, and a great and strong wind

rent the mountains, and brake in pieces the rocks before the LORD; but **the LORD was not in the wind:** *and after the wind an earthquake; but* **the LORD was not in the earthquake:** *[12] And after the earthquake a fire; but* **the LORD was not in the fire:** *and after the fire* <u>**a still small voice.**</u> *(1 Kings 19:11-12)*

For one example, both Jesus and the Apostle Paul had numerous opportunities to convey that we go to heaven when we die, but they never did, not even once. Are we to believe they somehow overlooked this important information for us? Wouldn't it have been easy enough for Jesus to have added the phrase [*in bracketed,* ***bold****,* <u>*underlined*</u> *words*] in just one of these places?

> *[2] In my Father's house are many mansions: if it were not so, I would have told you. I go to prepare a place for you* **[in heaven]**. *[3] And if I go and prepare a place for you* **[in heaven]**, *I will come again, and receive you unto myself; that where I am* **[in heaven]**, *there* **[in heaven]** *ye may be also. (John 14:2-3)*

We must be vigilant to read Scripture just as it appears and not attempt to interject or eliminate words to fit our beliefs or preconceived notions.

We need to be open to receive.

For us to fully grasp Scriptural truth, we must be open to receive it by:

- Being teachable;

> *The* **heart of the prudent getteth knowledge;** *and the ear of the wise seeketh knowledge. (Proverbs 18:15)*

*Wisdom is the principal thing; therefore **get wisdom: and with all thy getting get understanding.*** *(Proverbs 4:7)*

- Willing to uncover self-deception;

*[22] But **be ye doers of the word, and not hearers only, deceiving your own selves.** [26] If any man among you seem to be religious, and bridleth not his tongue, but deceiveth his own heart, this man's religion is vain.* *(James 1:22, 26)*

*For if a man think himself to be something, when he is nothing, **he deceiveth himself.*** *(Galatians 6:3)*

- Wanting fuller revelation;

*And ye shall know the truth, and **the truth shall make you free.*** *(John 8:32)*

*Howbeit when he, the **Spirit of truth,** is come, he **will guide you into all truth:** for he shall not speak of himself; but whatsoever he shall hear, that shall he speak: and he will shew you things to come.* *(John 16:13)*

- Seeing value in self-examination;

***Let us search and try our ways**, and turn again to the LORD.* *(Lamentations 3:40)*

***Examine yourselves**, whether ye be in the faith; prove your own selves. Know ye not your own selves, how that Jesus Christ is in you, except ye be reprobates?* *(2 Corinthians 13:5)*

- Becoming passionate for uncovering hidden mysteries and truths.

*For who hath known the mind of the Lord, that he may instruct him? But **we have the mind of Christ.** (1 Corinthians 2:16)*

*Even **the mystery** which hath been hid from ages and from generations, but **now is made manifest to his saints:** (Colossians 1:26)*

Meanings for certain terms we will use.

Our last item of agreement is to establish certain terms we will use when discussing Scripture. I have deliberately chosen a vernacular, a translation and terms that I believe will relate to the largest audience. Meanings of terms include but are not limited to:

- God also means *Yahweh, Yahuah, Yahuwah, Elohim*; the God of Abraham, Isaac and Jacob/Israel;
- Jesus, Jesus Christ, Christ also means *Yeshua, Yahusha, Messiah;* the only begotten Son of God;
- Spirit, Holy Spirit, Holy Ghost also means *Ruach ha Kodesh;* God's Holy Spirit;
- Lord means and embodies both God the Father and our Lord Jesus Christ;
- Man, men, mankind, also includes and means woman and women;
- Believer means one who believes in, has received, trusts, and belongs exclusively to Jesus Christ;
- Natural man also means mortal, carnal, flesh and blood, soulish (*sense*), rebellious man.

Now that we have reached agreement, we will begin to answer our questions beginning with, "Who am I?" We will follow topics under discussion with supporting Scripture to establish what is written.

Summary.

- God has promised to reveal mysteries and truths to us;
- We have to search for our answers as hidden treasures;
- Scripture isn't just read, but the Spirit reveals it to us;
- Just because something is supernatural does not mean it came from God;
- We are to try (*test*) the spirits;
- We must be "*of God*" to hear His words;
- No prophecy of Scripture is of any private interpretation;
- Prophecy came not by the will of man, but holy men of God were moved and spoke by the Spirit;
- God gives all Scripture by inspiration;
- Scriptural verses must harmonize with other verses;
- Matters in Scripture are established by two, three, or more witnesses;
- Men and translations are fallible;
- What *is not written* in Scripture can sometimes be just as important and powerful as what *is written*;
- Translators added the *italicized words* found in the King James Bible;
- We should not add or eliminate words to fit our beliefs;
- We must be open to receive Scriptural truth by being teachable, willing to uncover self-deception, wanting a fuller revelation, seeing value in self-examination, and becoming passionate for uncovering hidden mysteries and truths.

~ FOUR ~

Body, soul, heart, and spirit

To answer our question, "Who am I?" will require some understanding of how we were created and the different parts that make us who we are.

What are the body, soul, heart, and spirit?

Volumes have been written by men about the body, soul, heart, and spirit in an attempt to explain them but they are still often misunderstood. We frequently misapply these terms when discussing Scripture and this has led to much error and disagreement among believers.

Upon this foundation of misunderstanding, countless false doctrines have been "*inferred*" (*to conclude from reasoning rather than explicit statements*) instead of relying on the written word of Scripture. Something "*inferred*" can simply be an opinion based on the fallible intellect and reasoning of man. This is not unlike what happened in the Garden of Eden with the tree of knowledge of good and evil. In the Garden, man chose to look to his own intellect and reasoning for determining good and evil instead of obeying God.

The purpose of our study is not to debate these many explanations but to simplistically present what the written Scriptures record. When the devil tempted Jesus in the wilderness, both Jesus and the devil always referred to Scripture as "*it is written*" and never as, "*it is inferred*." The comparison between "written" and "inferred" can be contrasted as just referring to "*The Ten Commandments*" as the "*The Ten Suggestions*."

> *[4] But he answered and said,* **It is written** ... *[6] ... for* **it is written** ... *[7] ...* **It is written** *again ... [10] ... for* **it is written** ... *(Matthew 4:4, 6, 7, 10)*

The body.

At death, most believers and non-believers alike agree that the body returns to dust. Many believe that the soul and/or spirit (*consciousness*) leave the body at death and either ascends to heaven or descends to hell in an alive, conscious state. Later, we will see that neither of these beliefs about the soul and spirit has any foundational support in Scripture.

There are two bodies mentioned for believers. The first is a mortal or natural body to which we have been born; sown in corruption, meaning that it will eventually die, deteriorate and return to dust. The second body is an incorruptible, immortal, spiritual body and is what believers will take on when Christ returns to raise them to life again, *at* the resurrection, *if* they are in Christ. We will see that the body and soul are essential to each other and inseparably linked, meaning that we never see either one alive or dead without the other.

> *In the sweat of thy face shalt thou eat bread, till thou return unto the ground; for out of it wast thou taken:* **for dust thou art, and unto dust shalt thou return.** *(Genesis 3:19)*

*[38] But **God giveth it a body** as it hath pleased him, and to every seed his own body. [42] So also is the resurrection of the dead. It is **sown in corruption**; it is **raised in incorruption**: [43] It is **sown in dishonour**; it is **raised in glory**: it is **sown in weakness**; it is **raised in power**: [44] It is **sown a natural body**; it is **raised a spiritual body. There is a natural body**, and **there is a spiritual body**.* (1 Corinthians 15:38, 42-44)

*[52] In a moment, in the twinkling of an eye, at the last trump: for the trumpet shall sound, and **the dead shall be raised incorruptible**, and we shall be changed. [53] For this corruptible must put on **incorruption** [indestructibility], and **this mortal must put on immortality** [freedom from death].* (1 Corinthians 15:52-53)

Some equate a spiritual body to that of an apparition or ghost. Scripture shows the risen, resurrected Christ as not always appearing in His full glory when He manifested to His disciples in a closed room. They became frightened because they thought they saw a ghost. Jesus comforted them with His invitation to touch Him and see His flesh and bones. He also requested and ate food.

Because we are to be conformed to the image of the Son, our spiritual bodies appear to have flesh and bones and we might also eat food.

*And after eight days again his disciples were within, and Thomas with them: then **came Jesus, the doors being shut, and stood in the midst**, and said, Peace be unto you.* (John 20:26)

*[36] And as they thus spake, Jesus himself stood in the midst of them, and saith unto them, Peace be unto you. [37] But they were **terrified and affrighted**, and supposed **that they had seen a spirit**. [38] And he said unto them, Why are ye troubled? and why do thoughts arise in your*

hearts? [39] Behold my hands and my feet, that it is I myself: **handle me,** *and see;* **for a spirit hath not flesh and bones, as ye see me have.** *[40] And when he had thus spoken, he shewed them his hands and his feet. [41] And while they yet believed not for joy, and wondered, he said unto them,* **Have ye here any meat?** *[42] And they gave him a piece of a broiled fish, and of an honeycomb. [43]* **And he took it, and did eat before them.** *(Luke 24:36-43)*

For whom he did foreknow, he also did predestinate to be **conformed to the image of his Son,** *that he might be the firstborn among many brethren. (Romans 8:29)*

Our mortal bodies are formed within the womb from the dust, with all the elements and minerals from the earth that we need to sustain life.

The soul.

Many believe and teach that God puts a separate, additional attribute into man's body at the time of his creation called "*the soul*," but is this belief supported with clearly written Scripture?

> Strong's Old Testament Hebrew dictionary definition for Soul.
> Soul: H5315, *nephesh*: a living being, breathing creature, self, person, mind, own.

> Strong's New Testament Greek dictionary definition for Soul.
> Soul: G5590, *psuche*: distinct identity, unique personhood, individual personality, self, mind.

God formed man with everything he needed to be a man; a body by which he could move and have sensation or conscious experience; a mind and emotions for perceiving his experiences; and a will for creating and responding to experiences. Man had everything he needed to be man EXCEPT LIFE; the breath of life, power, animation, consciousness. Man was not given a soul as a separate attribute from the body but with the breath of life (*spirit*) from God, *"man became a living soul."*

> *And the LORD God formed man of the dust of the ground, and* **breathed** *into his nostrils the* **breath of life;** *and* **man became a living soul.** *(Genesis 2:7)*

> *Neither is worshipped with men's hands, as though he needed any thing, seeing* **he giveth to all life, and breath,** *and all things; (Acts 17:25)*

> Breath: G4157, *pnoe*: a respiration, a breeze, breath, wind.

The word soul is from the Hebrew word "*nephesh*" and means a creature with the breath of life or spirit. When this breath of life (*spirit*) is taken back by God, the "living soul" (*body/soul*) dies and is no longer conscious.

> *Thou hidest thy face, they are troubled:* **thou takest away their breath, they die,** *and* **return to their dust.** *(Psalms 104:29)*

> *And, behold, I, even I, do bring a flood of waters upon the earth, to destroy all flesh,* **wherein is the breath of life,** *from under heaven; and* **every thing** *that is in the earth* **shall die.** *(Genesis 6:17)*

> Breath: H7307, *ruach*: breath, wind, *life*, expression, function, air.
> Life: H2416, *chay*: alive, *life* or living thing.

Man and all other creatures have the same breath of life and mortality. How then is the *man-creature* different from the *other-creatures*? Man is made in the image of God: other creatures are not.

*For **that which befalleth the sons of men befalleth beasts;** even one thing befalleth them: as the one dieth, so dieth the other; yea, **they have all one breath;** so that a man hath no preeminence above a beast: for all is vanity. (Ecclesiastes 3:19).*

*So **God created man in his own image,** in the image of God created he him; male and female created he them. (Genesis 1:27)*

A soul can mean a person and is who and what we are; the self or our self.

We also call man's "*being*" or "*existence*" as "*soul.*" At the time of his death, man's body along with everything else of man; his thoughts, emotions, will, experiences, knowledge, wisdom, etc. (*the soul*) also perish and die.

*His **breath** goeth forth, he returneth to his earth; **in that very day his thoughts perish.** (Psalms 146:4)*

*Also **their love, and their hatred, and their envy, is now perished;** neither have they any more a portion for ever in any thing that is done under the sun. (Ecclesiastes 9:6)*

The teaching that man has an "*immortal soul*" is popularly taught today by the Catholic Church in their Catechism and by almost all Protestant Churches. The Evangelical Alliance confirmed their belief in the immortality of the soul at their first general conference in 1846.

"The Church teaches that every spiritual **soul** is created immediately by God – it is not "produced" by the parents – and also that **it is immortal: it does not perish when it separates from the body at death,** and it will be reunited with the body at the final Resurrection." (Paragraph No. 366, Catechism of the Catholic Church) "**the immortality of the soul,** the resurrection of the body, the judgment of the world by Jesus Christ, with the eternal blessedness of the righteous and the eternal punishment of the wicked;" (Point No. 8, The Evangelical Alliance – Points of Belief, Report of the First General Conference, 1846)

The belief that the soul separates from the body and continues to live at the moment of death is not found anywhere in Scripture but seems to have originated from ancient Greek philosophy by Socrates, Plato and Aristotle. Their philosophical reasoning is but one example to show that the very best of man's intellect and thinking, without God and revelation by His Spirit, will always be seriously flawed for coming to the knowledge of the truth.

*Ever learning, and **never able** to come to the knowledge of the truth. (2 Timothy 3:7)*

If we button a shirt and miss the first button, all the other buttons will be off. The outcome will be a sloppy garment that is recognizable by anyone who sees it. All of our attempts to straighten it will be useless. The only fix is to start over and button the shirt as intended. When man ignores Scripture about the inseparable link between body and soul, he misses the first button.

Now is a good time to ask ourselves, did we get our understanding of an immortal soul directly from our study of Scripture, or did we get it from the teachings of an organized religion, church, or another person we thought might know?

The heart.

The seat where the faculties of man reside is described as *"heart"* and includes the mind, emotions, and will; from which come intellect, reason, comprehension, imagination, memory, instinct, intuition, etc. We see that man can bring forth both good and evil out of the treasure of his heart. He speaks out of the condition of his heart, and in his tongue is the power of life and death. Our words can be extremely powerful for pronouncing both blessings and curses. Our heart can also deceive us.

> Strong's Old Testament Hebrew dictionary definition for Heart.
> Heart: H3820, *leb*: feelings, will, intellect, mind.

> Strong's New Testament Greek dictionary definition for Heart.
> Heart, G2588, *kardia*: thoughts, feelings, mind (mind, emotions, will), intention.

*A good man out of the good treasure of his **heart** bringeth forth that which is good; and an evil man out of the evil treasure of his **heart** bringeth forth that which is evil: for **of the abundance of the heart his mouth speaketh.** (Luke 6:45)*

*[20] And he said, That which cometh out of the man, that defileth the man. [21] For **from within, out of the heart** of men, proceed evil thoughts, adulteries, fornications, murders, [22] Thefts, covetousness, wickedness, deceit, lasciviousness, an evil eye, blasphemy, pride, foolishness: [23] All these evil things come from within, and defile the man. (Mark 7:20-23)*

For as he thinketh in his heart, so is he … (Proverbs 23:7)

***Death and life are in the power of the tongue:** and they that love it shall eat the fruit thereof. (Proverbs 18:21)*

*The **heart is deceitful above all things**, and desperately wicked: **who can know it?** (Jeremiah 17:9)*

Man's will determines what he does with the gift of life, and the condition of his heart *(his mind – what he thinks; his emotions – what he feels; and his will – what he desires and does)* determines his nature and the spirit *(life)* he will manifest and exhibit.

The spirit.

Scripture speaks about different spirits, including God's Holy Spirit and evil spirits. Here we will only be examining man's spirit.

At man's creation, aside from *"life,"* can it be found written anywhere in Scripture that God installed a separate, additional attribute into man called *"a spirit?"* The implication of the word *"spirit"* when describing man's creation is basically the "breath of life" from God to man in his natural, mortal body. This breath gives man consciousness or awareness of perception. Both the Hebrew and Greek words also translate *"spirit"* to *"breath"* or *"air."*

> Strong's Old Testament Hebrew dictionary definition for Spirit.
> Spirit: H7307, *ruach*: breath, wind, *life*, expression, function, air.

> Strong's New Testament Greek dictionary definition for Spirit.
> Spirit: G4151, *pneuma*: a current of air, breath, breeze, *life*, vital principle.

*The **Spirit of God** hath made me, and **the breath of the Almighty hath given me life**. (Job 33:4)*

*It **is the spirit that quickeneth**; the flesh profiteth nothing: the words that I speak unto you, they are spirit, and they are life. (John 6:63)*

Quickeneth: G2227, *zoopoieo*: vitalize, make alive, give life, empower with divine life.

The spirit is the life, and it has always belonged to God, the giver of all life, and not to man. Natural, mortal man has it only for a season, and when he dies, the "life" or "spirit" returns to God who gave it. Because spirit is life, the exact opposite of death, life does not die.

> **Then shall the dust return to the earth** *as it was: and the* **spirit shall return unto God** *who gave it. (Ecclesiastes 12:7)*

The spirit is also the "*expression*" or "*reflection*" of the inner self (*the soul*). Man manifests his natural sense or soul nature until the Holy Spirit manifests in his heart. Man cannot change the expression of who he is by his own strength. There has to be a change of heart and the change of heart can only come from God.

Regardless of what one chooses to believe about the body, soul, heart, and spirit, we are going to see that at the time of death, everything of man will perish and die; life is over. Man does NOT remain conscious (*alive*) but will sleep in an unconscious state until he is raised from his slumber at the resurrection.

It's interesting to note that fallen man in his pride and rebellion against God lays claim that the spirit (*life*) is his and belongs to him. Later, we will see why when we examine the *"BIG LIE."*

> *For ye are bought with a price: therefore glorify God in* **your body, and in your spirit, which are God's.** *(1 Corinthians 6:20)*

We can compare mortal man to a computer with all its components and software installed *(body/soul)*. The computer has everything it needs to function as a computer except power (*life* or *spirit*). Without power, the computer is unresponsive, but with power the computer boots to life and can do everything it was uniquely designed to do. Remove the power and the computer dies. Resurrect it by restoring power again and the computer snaps back to life along with all its amassed and stored data (*experiences*).

Summary.

- Both Jesus and the devil always referred to Scripture as *"it is written"* and never as *"it is inferred;"*
- God created man a *"living soul"* and did not put a separate soul into him;
- Our soul is our *self*;
- Today most churches teach that man's soul is immortal;
- Scripture teaches that man's soul is not immortal, it will die;
- Our heart includes our mind, emotions, and will;
- The spirit is the life and has always belonged to God, and not to man;
- Spirit is also the manifestation and reflection of man's heart;
- A change of heart has to come from God;
- Spirit is life and when man dies the life returns to God who gave it.

~ FIVE ~

From our beginning to death

In this chapter, we will find the answers to our next questions: "How did I get here?" and "What happens when I die?" We will be following the chronological path of man from his creation to his death and what is to follow. Let's begin with "How did I get here?"

In the beginning, God formed Adam into a living soul and gave him life.

Man was formed from the dust of the ground and became a living soul with the breath of life from God. We will also see that man shares the same breath of life and mortality with the animals.

> *And the LORD God formed man of the dust of the ground, and* **breathed** *into his nostrils the* **breath** *of life; and* **man became a living soul.** *(Genesis 2:7)*

Breathed: H5301, *naphach*: to breathe, blow.

Breath: H5397, *neshamah*: puff, wind, vital breath, divine inspiration, intellect.

Soul: H5315, *nephesh*: a living being, breathing creature, self, person, mind, own.

God warned Adam if he disobeyed and sinned, he would surely die.

Adam was given the legal precedent of "express notice," meaning that he was told very clearly what the consequences of disobeying God would be. He would surely die.

> *[16] And the LORD God commanded the man, saying, Of every tree of the garden thou mayest freely eat: [17] But of the tree of the knowledge of good and evil, thou shalt not eat of it: for in the day that thou eatest thereof **thou shalt surely die.** (Genesis 2:16-17)*

> *But of the fruit of the tree which is in the midst of the garden, **God hath said, Ye shall not eat of it, neither shall ye touch it, lest ye die.** (Genesis 3:3)*

The serpent (enemy) opposed God and lied to Eve.

The "father of lies," the serpent or enemy was there at the very beginning of man. He lied by proclaiming to the woman that they would not surely die.

> *And the serpent said unto the woman, **Ye shall not surely die:** (Genesis 3:4)*

Notice that the enemy didn't directly call God a liar. He only set the stage to make God appear as a liar in the mind of the woman. The enemy often sets us up to make our wrong mental jumps and conclusions.

Adam and Eve were driven out of the Garden of Eden.

God did not want us to live forever in sin because of its dire conse-quences. He has prepared a way of escape for us as we will later see. No sinner will naturally live forever apart from Jesus Christ.

> *[22] And the LORD God said, Behold, the man is become as one of us, to know good and evil: and now,* **lest he put forth his hand, and take also of the tree of life, and eat, and live for ever:** *[23] Therefore* **the LORD God sent him forth from the garden of Eden,** *to till the ground from whence he was taken. [24] So* **he drove out the man;** *and he placed at the east of the garden of Eden Cherubims, and* **a flaming sword which turned every way, to keep the way of the tree of life.** *(Genesis 3:22-24)*

After Adam had lived 930 years, he died.

> *And all the days that Adam lived were nine hundred and thirty years: and* **he died.** *(Genesis 5:5)*

The living soul that sins will die.

Living souls (*people*) will die just as God said would happen at the beginning. By the one man, Adam, sin came into the world and death passed to all men. God did not bring sin into the world, man did. We should remember the first sin the next time we want to blame God for all the evil in the world. By the obedience of one man, Jesus Christ, we can be made righteous and inherit immortality but it will be on God's terms and not our own.

> *[12] Wherefore, as* **by one man sin entered into the world, and death by sin;** *and so death passed upon all men, for that all have sinned. [19] For as by one man's disobedience many were made sinners, so by the obedience of one shall many be made righteous. (Romans 5:12, 19)*

Behold, all souls are mine; as the soul of the father, so also the soul of the son is mine: **the soul that sinneth, it shall die.** *(Ezekiel 18:4)*

The soul that sinneth, it shall die. *The son shall not bear the iniquity of the father, neither shall the father bear the iniquity of the son: the righteousness of the righteous shall be upon him, and the wickedness of the wicked shall be upon him. (Ezekiel 18:20)*

For the wages of sin is death; but the gift of God is eternal life through Jesus Christ our Lord. *(Romans 6:23)*

Death: G2288, *thanatos*: to die, separation from life.
Eternal: G166, *aionios*: perpetual, eternal, forever.

Souls are people.

By definition, souls are any living, breathing, mortal creature. At some early time, it appears a decision was made to call people souls.

And all the **souls** *that came out of the loins of Jacob were* **seventy souls:** *for Joseph was in Egypt already. (Exodus 1:5)*

Then they that gladly received his word were baptized: and the same day there were added unto them about **three thousand souls.** *(Acts 2:41)*

Which sometime were disobedient, when once the longsuffering of God waited in the days of Noah, while the ark was a preparing, wherein few, that is, **eight souls** *were saved by water. (1 Peter: 3:20)*

All have sinned.

Since Adam, everyone has been born into the original sin. Original sin also includes the most innocent baby being born at this very moment.

> *For all have sinned, and come short of the glory of God; (Romans 3:23)*

> *Wherefore, as by one man sin entered into the world, and death by sin; and so **death passed upon all men,** for that **all have sinned:** (Romans 5:12)*

We saw how God created the first man and instructed him how to live forever by the tree of life in the Garden of Eden. We also saw that the first man's disobedience to God brought death upon all men, but by the obedience of one man, Jesus Christ, we can be made righteous and inherit immortality. Now we will examine "What happens when I die?"

The Spirit is the breath that gives life: flesh dies with the removal of breath.

The breath of life from God is also called spirit. With the breath of life, we become alive. When God gathers the breath back to Himself, we die. The same is also true for beasts.

> *All the while my **breath** is in me, and the **spirit of God is in my nostrils;** (Job 27:3)*

Breath: H5397, *neshamah*: puff, wind, vital breath, divine inspiration, intellect.
Spirit: H7307, *ruach*: breath, wind, *life*, expression, function, air.

Nostrils: H639, *aph*: a nostril, nose.

*The **Spirit of God** hath made me, and **the breath of the Almighty hath given me life.** (Job 33:4)*

*Neither is worshipped with men's hands, as though he needed any thing, seeing **he giveth to all life, and breath,** and all things; (Acts 17:25)*

*[14] If he set his heart upon man, **if he gather unto himself his spirit and his breath;** [15] **All flesh shall perish** together, and **man shall turn again unto dust.** (Job 34:14-15)*

*For **that which befalleth the sons of men befalleth beasts;** even one thing befalleth them: as the one dieth, so dieth the other; yea, **they have all one breath;** so that a man hath no preeminence above a beast: for all is vanity. (Ecclesiastes 3:19).*

The dead are unconscious and know not anything; everything a part of them dies.

When someone dies, everything else about them dies too. That person's thoughts, emotions, memories, work, intelligence, knowledge, and wisdom also perish and die.

*[5] For the living know that they shall die: but **the dead know not any thing,** neither have they any more a reward; for the memory of them is forgotten. [6] Also **their love, and their hatred, and their envy, is now perished;** neither have they any more a portion for ever in any thing that is done under the sun. (Ecclesiastes 9:5-6)*

*His **breath** goeth forth, he returneth to his earth; **in that very day his thoughts perish.** (Psalms 146:4)*

Dead: H4191, *muth*: to die, to be dead.
Breath: H7307, *ruach*: breath, wind, *life*, expression, function, air.
Perish: H6, *abad*: annihilated, destroyed, lost.

*[4] Return, O LORD, deliver my soul: oh save me for thy mercies' sake. [5] For **in death there is no remembrance of thee:** in the grave who shall give thee thanks? (Psalms 6:4-5)*

*The **dead praise not the LORD, neither any that go down into silence.** (Psalms 115:17)*

Silence: H1745, *dumah*: to be dumb, figuratively death.

*For the **grave** cannot praise thee, **death can not celebrate thee:** they that go down into the pit cannot hope for thy truth. (Isaiah 38:18)*

Grave: H7585, *sheol*: hades, the world of the dead, hell, pit.
Death: H4194, *maveth*: the dead, their place or state (hades).

There is no work, device, knowledge, or wisdom in the grave.

*Whatsoever thy hand findeth to do, do it with thy might; for there is **no work, nor device, nor knowledge, nor wisdom, in the grave,** whither thou goest. (Ecclesiastes 9:10)*

Device: H2808, cheshbon: contrivance, intelligence, reason.

The dead cannot return to haunt their house or any other place.

If it's not the dead haunting, then who is it? These are evil spirits that we will discuss a little later.

> *[9] As the cloud is consumed and vanisheth away: so **he that goeth down to the grave shall come up no more.** [10] **He shall return no more to his house,** neither shall his place know him any more. (Job 7:9-10)*

The soul is not immortal. Scripture calls man mortal.

The living soul is not immortal and never has been. Immortality comes for believers at the resurrection when Christ returns and not at the time of death.

> Strong's Old Testament Hebrew dictionary definition for Mortal.
> Mortal: H582, *enosh*: a mortal, man, mankind.

> Strong's New Testament Greek dictionary definition for Mortal.
> Mortal: G2349, *thnetos*: subject to death, liable to die.

> *Shall **mortal man** be more just than God? shall a man be more pure than his maker? (Job 4:17)*

> *For we which live are alway delivered unto death for Jesus' sake, that the life also of Jesus might be made manifest in our **mortal flesh**. (2 Corinthians 4:11)*

Because of sin, mortal man will return to dust.

Mortal man has an appointed destiny to die once and return to the dust (*earth*). Only those who are alive and "caught up" when Christ returns for the resurrection appear to escape death as we will see in the next chapter "The Resurrection of the Dead."

*In the sweat of thy face shalt thou eat bread, till thou return unto the ground; for out of it wast thou taken: **for dust thou art, and unto dust shalt thou return.** (Genesis 3:19)*

Dust: *aphar*, H6083: dust, clay, earth.

Remember, I beseech thee, that thou hast made me as the clay; and wilt thou bring me into dust again? (Job 10:9)

They shall go down to the bars of the pit, when our rest together is in the dust. (Job 17:16)

Pit: H7585, *sheol*: hades, the world of the dead, hell, grave.

*And as **it is appointed unto men once to die,** but after this the judgment: (Hebrews 9:27)*

Death is the creation of a living soul in reverse.

Man became alive when God breathed the breath of life (*spirit*) into the dust He formed.

- ***Dust + Spirit = Life.***

*And the LORD God formed man of the dust of the ground, and **breathed** into his nostrils the **breath of life;** and **man became a living soul.** (Genesis 2:7)*

When man dies, the dust returns to the earth and the breath of life (*spirit*) returns to God.

- ***Dust – Spirit = Death.***

Then shall the dust return to the earth as it was: and the spirit shall return unto God who gave it. (Ecclesiastes 12:7)

Thou hidest thy face, they are troubled: thou takest away their breath, they die, and return to their dust. (Psalms 104:29)

Only Jesus Christ, the *King of kings* and *Lord of lords,* has immortality.

After Jesus Christ was crucified, died, and was buried, God raised Him to life again with immortality. A resurrection is required to have life again.

*[14] That thou keep this commandment without spot, unrebukeable, until the appearing of **our Lord Jesus Christ:** [15] Which in his times he shall shew, who is **the blessed and only Potentate, the King of kings, and Lord of lords;** [16] <u>**Who only hath immortality,**</u> dwelling in the light which no man can approach unto; whom no man hath seen, nor can see: to whom be honour and power everlasting. Amen. (1 Timothy 6:14-16)*

Immortality: G110, *athanasia*: immortality, deathlessness.

*For God so loved the world, that he gave his only begotten Son, that **whosoever believeth in him should not perish, but have everlasting life.** (John 3:16)*

Jesus Christ abolished death and brought life and immortality through the gospel.

The gospel proclaims our great hope and promise of salvation. The good news of the gospel is that God has prepared a way for us to achieve victory over the greatest enemy of all, death. Is there anyone who does not want to live forever?

*But is now made manifest by the appearing of our Saviour **Jesus Christ, who hath abolished death**, and **hath brought life and immortality** to light **through the gospel**: (2 Timothy 1:10)*

*Verily, verily, I say unto you, **He that believeth on me hath everlasting life**. (John 6:47)*

Believers have come to the knowledge of the truth. We understand that immortality can be ours by God's all-sufficient grace, but we are required to seek it. We seek it by confessing with our mouth, believing in our heart, and calling upon the name of the Lord Jesus Christ to be saved.

*To them who by patient continuance in well doing **seek for** glory and honour and **immortality, eternal life**: (Romans 2:7)*

Immortality: G861, *aphtharsia:* unending existence, indestructibility.

*[9] That **if thou shalt confess with thy mouth** the Lord Jesus, and shalt **believe in thine heart** that God hath raised him from the dead, **thou shalt be saved**. [10] For with the heart man believeth unto righteousness; and with the mouth confession is made unto salvation. [11] For the scripture saith, Whosoever believeth on him shall not be ashamed. [13] For **whosoever shall call upon the name of the Lord shall be saved**. (Romans 10:9-11, 13)*

*[8] For **by grace are ye saved through faith**; and that not of yourselves: it is the gift of God: [9] Not of works, lest any man should boast. (Ephesians 2:8-9)*

What then is death?

Throughout Scripture, sleep is consistently the image used for death.

Strong's Old Testament Hebrew dictionary definition for Sleep.
Sleep: H3462, *yashen*: sleep (figurative to die).

Strong's New Testament Greek dictionary definition for Sleep.
Sleep: G2837, *koimao*: sleep, be dead.

[11] These things said he: and after that he saith unto them, Our friend Lazarus **sleepeth***; but I go, that I may awake him out of* **sleep***. [12] Then said his disciples, Lord, if he sleep, he shall do well. [13] Howbeit* **Jesus spake of his death: but they thought that he had spoken of taking of rest in sleep***. [14]* **Then said Jesus unto them plainly,** <u>**Lazarus is dead**</u>*. (John 11:11-14)*

Sleepeth: G2837, *koimao*: sleep, be dead.
Dead: G599, *apothnesko*: to die.

Job describes that if he had died, he would have slept. Then he speaks about being at rest. Old tombstones frequently carried the inscription, "R.I.P" for *rest in peace.*

For now should I have lain still and been quiet, **I should have slept***: then had I been* **at rest***, (Job 3:13)*

[17] There the wicked cease from troubling; and there **the weary be at rest***. [18] There* **the prisoners rest together***; they hear not the voice of the oppressor. [19] The small and great are there; and the servant is free from his master. (Job 3:17-19)*

So **man lieth down, and riseth not***: till the heavens be no more,* **they shall not awake, nor be raised out of their sleep***. (Job 14:12)*

Consider and hear me, O LORD my God: lighten mine eyes, **lest I sleep the sleep of death***; (Psalms 13:3)*

Sleep: H3462, *yashen*: sleep, (figurative to die).
Death: H4194, *maveth*: the dead, their place or state (hades), ruin.

*And many of **them that sleep in the dust of the earth** shall awake, some to everlasting life, and some to shame and everlasting contempt. (Daniel 12:2)*

*[59] And they stoned Stephen, calling upon God, and saying, Lord Jesus, **receive my spirit**. [60] And he kneeled down, and cried with a loud voice, Lord, lay not this sin to their charge. And when he had said this, **he fell asleep**. (Acts 7:59-60)*

The Apostle Paul constantly used the expression "*sleep*" to describe the condition of the dead. Paul understood that those who were fallen asleep had died and perished.

*For this cause many are weak and sickly among you, and **many sleep**. (1 Corinthians 11:30)*

*After that, he was seen of above five hundred brethren at once; of whom the greater part remain unto this present, but **some are fallen asleep**. (1 Corinthians 15:6)*

*[17] And if Christ be not raised, your faith is vain; ye are yet in your sins. [18] Then **they also which are fallen asleep** in Christ **are perished**. (1 Corinthians 15:17-18)*

*Behold, I shew you a mystery; **We shall not all sleep**, but we shall all be changed, (1 Corinthians 15:51)*

Sleep, Asleep: G2837, *koimao*: sleep, be dead.

From what we have now seen of the dead as described in Scripture, they have not gone anywhere as alive and conscious after they died but are at rest.

Summary.

- In the beginning, God formed Adam into a living soul and breathed life into him;
- God warned Adam if he sinned by eating from the tree of knowledge of good and evil, he would surely die;
- The enemy lied to the woman by saying they would not surely die;
- Adam and Eve were driven out of the Garden of Eden when they sinned;
- The living soul that sins will die because the wages of sin is death;
- Souls are people;
- All have sinned;
- The Spirit is the breath that gives life: flesh dies with the removal of breath: The living soul is not immortal;
- Jesus Christ abolished death and brought life through the gospel;
- Man can achieve immortality, but it will be on God's terms;
- Scripture refers to death as sleep.

~ SIX ~

The resurrection of the dead

In the previous chapter, we have already seen the condition of the dead as:

- Asleep;
- Unconscious;
- Without life;
- Without thoughts and emotions.

The dead don't know anything.

> *... **the dead know not any thing** ... (Ecclesiastes 9:5)*

Jesus Christ's first coming two-thousand years ago was the most important event in all of history at that time. His next or second coming for the resurrection is the next most important event ever in the history of mankind.

Resurrection means bringing the dead to life again. Resurrection, a difficult concept for man to accept in the time of Christ, remains so today. People saw with their own eyes when Jesus raised the dead to life again and still would not believe. Only with faith can one accept the concept of resurrection. Jesus taught a resurrection of the dead. He would later die and be resurrected to life again to show man that the only way to immortality will be through Him.

> *Now faith is the substance of things hoped for, the evidence of things not seen. (Hebrews 11:1)*

> *While **we look** not at the things which are seen, but **at the things which are not seen**: for the things which are seen are temporal; but **the things which are not seen are eternal**. (2 Corinthians 4:18)*

> *[31] But as touching **the resurrection of the dead**, have ye not read that which was spoken unto you by God, saying, [32] I am the God of Abraham, and the God of Isaac, and the God of Jacob? **God is not the God of the dead, but of the living**. (Matthew 22:31-32)*

The death and resurrection of Jesus.

The Scriptures teach that Jesus would be killed, buried, and raised to life again. He now has the keys of hell (*grave*) and death, the power of man's immortality.

> *From that time forth began Jesus to shew unto his disciples, how that he must go unto Jerusalem, and suffer many things of the elders and chief priests and scribes, and **be killed, and be raised again** the third day. (Matthew 16:21)*

*[3] For I delivered unto you first of all that which I also received, how that **Christ died for our sins** according to the scriptures; [4] And that **he was buried, and that he rose again the third** day according to the scriptures: (1 Corinthians 15:3-4)*

***I am he that liveth, and was dead**; and, behold, **I am alive for evermore**, Amen; and **have the keys of hell and of death**. (Revelation 1:18)*

*And unto the angel of the church in Smyrna write; These things saith **the first and the last, which was dead, and is alive**; (Revelation 2:8)*

All the dead will be resurrected, both the just and the unjust.

The Scriptures layout the details of what occurs after death and summarize two very different destinies for us. When we are raised from the dead, everyone will hear His voice. What is not said is those who have done good ("*the just*") and those who have done evil ("*the unjust*"), will be resurrected at the same time. We will see that "the just" are resurrected when Christ returns, "the unjust" a thousand years later for judgment.

*[28] Marvel not at this: for the hour is coming, in the which **all that are in the graves shall hear his voice, [29] And shall come forth; they that have done good, unto the resurrection of life; and they that have done evil, unto the resurrection of damnation.** (John 5:28-29)*

*And many of them that sleep in the dust of the earth shall awake, **some to everlasting life**, and **some to shame and everlasting contempt**. (Daniel 12:2)*

And have hope toward God, which they themselves also allow, that **there shall be a resurrection of the dead, both of the just and unjust**. *(Acts 24:15)*

Often, these verses can be taken out of context to suggest that resurrection will occur at the same time for all, but they wouldn't harmonize with other Scripture. Jesus will judge the quick (*alive*) and the dead (*in Christ*) at His appearing and kingdom when He returns for the resurrection.

I charge thee therefore before God, and the Lord Jesus Christ, who shall judge the quick [alive] and the **dead at his appearing and his kingdom**; *(2 Timothy 4:1)*

[10] For **we must all appear before the judgment seat of Christ**; *that every one may receive the things done in his body, according to that he hath done, whether it be good or bad. [17] Therefore* **if any man be in Christ, he is a new creature: old things are passed away; behold, all things are become new**. *(2 Corinthians 5:10, 17)*

There is an order to the resurrection.

The beginning of the "first resurrection" appears to have started when Jesus Christ was raised from the dead and became the "*firstfruits*" of them that slept (*the dead*). He opened the way for the resurrection of all who believe in Him. Scripture states there is an order to the resurrection: 1) first is Christ; 2) afterward every man in his own order.

[20] But now is **Christ risen from the dead, and become the firstfruits of them that slept.** *[21] For since by man came death, by man came also the* **resurrection** *of the dead. [22] For as in Adam all die, even so* **in Christ shall all be made alive. [23] But every man in his own order: Christ the firstfruits; afterward they that are Christ's at his coming**. *(1 Corinthians 15:20-23)*

Resurrection: G386, *anastasis*: raised to life again, rise from the dead.

Coming: G3952, *parousia*: presence, arrival, advent, return.

It's going to be important in our study to remember that the time when believers will be resurrected or raised from the dead will be **at His coming.** Scripture also refers to this event as:

- At His coming;
- The coming of the Lord;
- The coming of our Lord Jesus Christ;
- When He shall appear;
- At the last day;
- The end;
- At the end of days.

After Jesus' resurrection, many bodies of dead saints also arose out of their graves and appeared unto many in the holy city. They also need to be included in our consideration of the first resurrection.

Scripture makes no mention that these saints/souls (or as some erroneously call their "*spirits*") had gone to heaven when they died and came back down to re-inhabit their bodies before they arose. Instead, the saints experienced resurrection from the grave (*awakened from their sleep*). Scripture doesn't elaborate further about what happened to them but it's reasonable to conclude that they didn't go back to their graves or their homes. Perhaps they were also resurrected as part of the "*firstfruits*" after Christ. Scripture often compares the harvest of souls to an agricultural harvest. The spring "Feast of Firstfruits" follows the holy convocations of "Passover" and the "Feast of Unleavened Bread."

*[52] And **the graves were opened; and many bodies of the saints which slept arose**, [53] And **came out of the graves after his resurrection**, and went into the holy city, and **appeared unto many** (Matthew 27:52-53).*

Speak unto the children of Israel, and say unto them, When ye be come into the land which I give unto you, and shall reap the harvest thereof, then **ye shall bring a sheaf of the firstfruits of your harvest** *unto the priest: (Leviticus 23:10)*

The mention of the holy city could have been the physical city of Jerusalem. Their appearing from graves would certainly have witnessed the teachings of Christ about the resurrection of the dead. Spiritually speaking, the "holy city" is "new Jerusalem," "the bride of Christ." Scripture does not specify the "many" to whom they appeared.

And I John saw the **holy city**, **new Jerusalem**, *coming down from God out of heaven, prepared* **as a bride** *adorned for her husband. (Revelation 21:2)*

When Christ returns, the order becomes:

- Those who sleep, the dead believers in Christ rise first, then;
- Those alive, the living believers are caught up together with them in the clouds;
- They meet the Lord in the air;
- They return with Him back down to the earth for His thousand year reign.

The dead in Christ rise (*are resurrected*) first, then those who are alive and remain are "caught up" (*they are changed but not said to be resurrected*) together with them to meet the Lord in the air. Notice what is not written and not said is that they go to be with Jesus Christ in heaven. What is written and said is that we will be with Him, wherever that might be.

There are some false doctrines that teach "*… them also which sleep in Jesus will God bring with him*" to mean the souls who died and went to heaven will return with Jesus from heaven for the resurrection of their bodies. Scripture doesn't speak to this notion at all but instead that both the resurrected and alive believers will meet Christ in the air before returning down to the earth. They will live and reign with Him for a thousand years on the earth, not in heaven.

> *[13] But I would not have you to be ignorant, brethren, concerning them which are asleep, that ye sorrow not, even as others which have no hope. [14] For if we believe that Jesus died and rose again, even so **them also which sleep in Jesus will God bring with him**. [15] For this we say unto you by the word of the Lord, that we which are alive and remain unto the coming of the Lord shall not prevent [precede] them which are asleep. [16] For the Lord himself shall descend from heaven with a shout, with the voice of the archangel, and with the trump of God: and **the dead in Christ shall rise first**: [17] **Then we which are alive and remain shall be caught up together with them in the clouds, to meet the Lord in the air: and so shall we ever be with the Lord.***
> *(1 Thessalonians 4:13-17)*

Asleep: G2837, *koimao*: sleep, be dead.
Prevent: G5348, *phthano*: to be beforehand, precede.
Descend: G2597, *katabaino*: come (get, go, step) down.
Shout: G2752, *keleuma*: a word of command, a call, an arousing outcry.
Voice: G5456, *phone*: disclosure, address, sound, noise.
Trump: G4536, *salpigx*: reverberation, trumpet, the sound of a trumpet.
Caught up: G726, *harpazo*: to seize, catch (away, up), pluck, pull, take.

> *[4]… **they lived and reigned with Christ a thousand years**. [5] But the rest of the dead lived not again until the thousand years were finished. **This is the first resurrection**. [6] Blessed and holy is he that hath part in the **first resurrection**: on such the second death hath no power,*

WHAT HAPPENS WHEN WE DIE?

*but **they shall be priests of God and of Christ, and shall reign with him a thousand years**. (Revelation 20:4-6)*

*And hast made us unto our God **kings and priests:** and **we shall reign on the earth**. (Revelation 5:10)*

*But the rest of the dead lived not again until the thousand years were finished. **This is the first resurrection**. (Revelation 20:5)*

God has placed man to live on the earth and not in heaven.

*The heaven, even the heavens, are the LORD'S: but **the earth hath he given to the children of men**. (Psalms 115:16)*

The first resurrection.

Scripture specifically names the event of Christ's return for the resurrection of believers as the "first resurrection." Those who have a part in it are called "blessed and holy" and the second death has no power over them because they have been changed. Because mortal man cannot inherit the kingdom of God, all believers must be changed at the resurrection when Christ returns. They must "put on" incorruption (*indestructibility*) and immortality (*freedom from death*).

In the next chapter, we will examine the next or second resurrection that follows the "first resurrection." Scripture doesn't specifically name it the "second resurrection" but we will use that term to refer to it.

How will Jesus Christ appear and come?

We will see that Jesus Christ ***appears and comes*** as:

- Faithful and True;
- The Word of God;

- King of kings and Lord of lords;
- Chief Shepherd;
- Our Lord Jesus Christ;
- The blessed and only Potentate;
- The Son of man;
- The Lord.

His "appearing" and "coming" are the same event and clearly established with two witnesses:

> *… at the mouth of two witnesses, or at the mouth of three witnesses, shall the matter be established. (Deuteronomy 19:15)*

1 Thessalonians 4:16-17:
"… the Lord himself shall descend from heaven …"
"… with the trump [trumpet] of God …"
"… dead in Christ … rise first; then we which are alive and remain … caught up …"

1 Corinthians 15:50-54:
"… We shall not all sleep, but we shall all be changed …"
"… at the last trump …"
"… mortal puts on immortality …"
"Death is swallowed up in victory."

We see other examples of how His coming was described in the "Olivet Discourse" for the events of that day:

Matthew 24:30-31:
"… they shall see the Son of man coming …"
"… with a great sound of a trumpet …"
"… the angels shall gather together His elect …"

Mark 13:26-27, 30
"… then shall they see the Son of man coming …"
"… then shall he send his angels, and shall gather together His elect …"
"… this generation shall not pass, till all these things be done."

The trumpet sounds at the same time:

- The Son of man comes;
- A shout, with the voice of the archangel;
- The Lord Himself shall descend from heaven;
- When the dead in Christ rise to meet the Lord in the air;
- When those alive are caught up together to meet the Lord in the air;
- When we shall be changed to put on incorruption and immortality;
- When we shall ever be with the Lord.

*[11] And **I saw heaven opened, and behold a white horse; and he that sat upon him was called Faithful and True**, and in righteousness he doth judge and make war. [13] And he was clothed with a vesture dipped in blood: and **his name is called The Word of God**. [16] And he hath on his vesture and on his thigh **a name written, KING OF KINGS, AND LORD OF LORDS**. (Revelation 19:11, 13, 16)*

*[14] That thou keep this commandment without spot, unrebukeable, until the **appearing** of **our Lord Jesus Christ**: [15] Which in his times he shall shew, who is **the blessed and only Potentate, the King of kings, and Lord of lords**; (1 Timothy 6:14-15)*

*And when the **chief Shepherd shall appear**, ye shall receive a crown of glory that fadeth not away. (1 Peter 5:4)*

And now, little children, abide in him; that, **when he shall ap-**
pear*, we may have confidence, and not be ashamed before him* **at his**
coming*. (1 John 2:28)*

For this we say unto you by the word of the Lord, that we which are
alive and remain unto the **coming of the Lord** *... (1 Thessalonians 4:15)*

What happens to those resurrected when Christ appears and comes?

Believers are changed at the resurrection when Christ returns.
Death (*of the mortal*) is swallowed up in victory (*by immortality*). This
change happens instantaneously, in a moment, in the twinkling of an
eye "at the last trump."

[50] Now this I say, brethren, that **flesh and blood cannot inher-**
it the kingdom of God*; neither doth corruption inherit incorruption.*
[51] Behold, I shew you a mystery; **We shall not all sleep, but we shall**
all be changed*, [52] In a moment, in the twinkling of an eye,* **at the**
last trump*: for the trumpet shall sound, and* **the dead shall be raised**
incorruptible*, and we shall be changed. [53] For this corruptible must*
put on **incorruption** *[indestructibility], and* **this mortal must put on**
immortality*. [54] So when this corruptible shall have put on incorrup-*
tion, and this **mortal shall have put on immortality***, then shall be*
brought to pass the saying that is written, **Death is swallowed up in**
victory*. (1 Corinthians 15:50-54)*

Raised: G1453, *egeiro*: to waken, to rouse from sleep or death.
Incorruptible: G862, *aphitartos*: indestructible, imperishable, immortal.
Corruptible: G5349, *phthartos*: decayed, perishable.
Incorruption: G861, *aphtharsia*: unending existence, indestructibility,
immortality.
Immortality: G110, *athanasia*: deathlessness, imperishability, freedom
from death.
Victory: G3534, *nikos*: a conquest, triumph.

85

Jesus promised that He would raise to life (*resurrect*) all that had been given to Him at the "last day." Again, many argue that this time is to resurrect only the body, but people base this on the false belief that the soul is immortal and lives on after the death of the body. We have already seen that the body and soul are inseparably linked, meaning that we never see one alive or dead without the other. As we examine this in context, the resurrection is to raise souls (*people*) to life again and not just dead bodies.

There is much debate about whether our old physical bodies will be raised as new spiritual bodies, or whether we will get a completely new spiritual body. Scripture seems to lean in the direction that our old, vile bodies will be changed to new, glorious ones. We can be at peace in the promise that we will have a spiritual body, period.

*[38] But **God giveth it a body** as it hath pleased him, and to every seed his own body. [42] So also is the resurrection of the dead. It is **sown in corruption**; it is **raised in incorruption**: [43] It is **sown in dishonour**; it is **raised in glory**: it is **sown in weakness**; it is **raised in power**: [44] It is **sown a natural body**; it is **raised a spiritual body**. There is a natural body, and **there is a spiritual body**. (1 Corinthians 15:38, 42-44)*

*[20] For our conversation is in heaven; from whence also we look for the Saviour, the Lord Jesus Christ: [21] **Who shall change our vile body, that it may be fashioned like unto his glorious body**, according to the working whereby he is able even to subdue all things unto himself. (Philippians 3:20-21)*

*[39] And this is the Father's will which hath sent me, that of all which he hath given me I should lose nothing, but should **raise it up again at the last day**. [40] And this is the will of him that sent me, that*

every one which seeth the Son, and believeth on him, may have everlasting life: and **I will raise him up at the last day.** *(John 6:39-40)*

[23] Jesus saith unto her, Thy brother shall rise again. [24] Martha saith unto him, **I know that he shall rise again in the resurrection at the last day.** *[25] Jesus said unto her,* **I am the resurrection, and the life**: *he that believeth in me, though he were dead, yet shall he live: [26] And* **whosoever liveth and believeth in me shall never die.** *Believest thou this? (John 11:23-26)*

What destiny awaits those who have a part in the first resurrection?

- They are raised at the last day;
- There is a sound of a trumpet;
- The dead are raised as incorruptible;
- Those alive are caught up with them in the air;
- They are all changed, in a moment, in the twinkling of an eye;
- The corruptible puts on incorruption (indestructibility);
- The mortal puts on immortality (freedom from death);
- Death is swallowed up in victory;
- They meet the Lord in the air;
- They return with Him to the earth;
- They will receive a crown of glory that never fades away;
- They shall ever be with the Lord;
- They shall be priests of God and Christ;
- They shall be kings and priests unto God;
- They shall reign with Him a thousand years;
- They shall reign on the earth.

We saw that the resurrection is the next, single most important event ever for those who have put their faith and trust in the promises of the Lord. Believers are going to be raised as immortal to live and reign as priests of God and Christ.

In the next chapter, we will examine what happens to those souls (*people*) who were not included in the first resurrection, but are resurrected a thousand years later to stand before God for judgment.

Summary.

- Jesus Christ's first coming was the most important event in all of history at that time. His next or second coming for the resurrection is the next most important event ever in the history of mankind;
- Jesus taught a resurrection of the dead;
- There will be a resurrection of the dead, both "*the just*" and "*the unjust*;"
- There is an order to the resurrection;
- Jesus died and was resurrected from the dead to become the *firstfruits* of them that sleep;
- The just will be resurrected when Christ returns and they put on indestructibility and immortality.

~ SEVEN ~

What follows the thousand year reign?

When is the next or second resurrection?
The event that seems to divide what Scripture has specifi-cally named the *first resurrection* and the second resurrection, when those not in Christ are raised for judgment, appears to follow the thousand year reign of Christ. At this time, the sea and death and hell (*hades*) give up their dead.

The word "hell" is not defined in Scripture as a place of eternal, fiery torment but most often as the place of the "unseen;" *sheol* in Hebrew and *hades* in Greek. Grave, pit and hell are words often used interchangeably and are identified in the same verse with the second death.

> Strong's Old Testament Hebrew dictionary definition for Hell.
> Hell: H7585, *sheol*: hades, the world of the dead, hell, pit.

> Strong's New Testament Greek dictionary definition for Hell.

Hell: G86, *hades*: the unseen place, invisible realm, present dwelling place of departed souls, grave.

Those who were not resurrected during the first resurrection will stand before God; He will judge them according to their works from a great white throne. Whosoever is not found written in the book of life will be cast into the lake of fire.

*[11] And I saw **a great white throne**, and him that sat on it, from whose face the earth and the heaven fled away; and there was found no place for them. [12] And **I saw the dead, small and great, stand before God; and the books were opened: and another book was opened, which is the book of life: and the dead were judged out of those things which were written in the books, according to their works**. [13] And **the sea gave up the dead which were in it; and death and hell delivered up the dead which were in them: and they were judged every man according to their works**. (Revelation 20:11-13)*

*[14] And **death and hell were cast into the lake of fire**. This is the second death. [15] **And whosoever was not found written in the book of life was cast into the lake of fire**. (Revelation 20:14-15)*

The "fearful" and the "unbelieving" are named with the abominable, murderers, whoremongers, sorcerers, idolaters, and liars.

*But **the fearful, and unbelieving**, and the abominable, and murderers, and whoremongers, and sorcerers, and idolaters, and all liars, **shall have their part in the lake** which burneth with fire and brimstone: which is the second death. (Revelation 21:8)*

What happens to those who have their part in the lake of fire?

Following the second resurrection, it might appear that those who have their part in the lake of fire will either suffer annihilation or burn forever in torment and agony. While this is frequent teaching, it does not begin to harmonize with the rest of Scripture. It also denies God's unconditional love for man and portrays Him as a monster who will burn His children alive to suffer perpetually. It could take a separate book to refute what man has made complicated about God's plan for the fulfillment and restoration of His creation. For brevity, I am going to super-condense some of the major points.

I once wrongly believed that the book of Revelation was a literal prophecy about end time events. Instead, it is symbolic and has spiritual meaning and application. To "signify" is to make known by signs and symbols;

> *... and he sent and **signified** it by his angel unto his servant John: (Revelation 1:1)*

The purpose of judgment is so the inhabitants of the world will learn righteousness or *"right-doing,"* that which is good and right in God's sight;

> *With my soul have I desired thee in the night; yea, with my spirit within me will I seek thee early: for **when thy judgments are in the earth, the inhabitants of the world will learn righteousness.** (Isaiah 26:9)*

Burning fire removes iniquity (*evil*) and purges sin but does not burn the sinner. When Isaiah saw the LORD of hosts, he realized his uncleanness. Fire purged Isaiah's sin and removed his iniquity, but he came to no harm;

*[5] Then said I, **Woe is me! for I am undone; because I am a man of unclean lips**, and I dwell in the midst of a people of unclean lips: for mine eyes have seen the King, the LORD of hosts. [6] Then flew one of the seraphims unto me, **having a live coal in his hand**, which he had taken with the tongs from off the altar: [7] **And he laid it upon my mouth, and said, Lo, this hath touched thy lips; and thine iniquity is taken away, and thy sin purged**. (Isaiah 6:5-7)*

God has shown Himself to be a consuming fire throughout Scripture;

*For our **God is** a consuming **fire**. (Hebrews 12:29)*

The lake of fire is not a real, literal fire but a symbolic fire of God that will burn and destroy all sin and consume the "works of the flesh." This is why unrepentant sinners came to have their part in the lake of fire in the first place. Having these sinful and carnal passions purified by the consuming fire of God's Holy Spirit can be an agonizing and tormenting experience for the sinner, but it doesn't last forever. All sin and evil must be destroyed for the fulfillment and restoration of His creation. This purging is the second death, the death of all sin. It is the final judgment;

*[7] But the heavens and the earth, which are now, by the same word are kept in store, **reserved unto fire against the day of judgment and perdition of ungodly men** [10] But the day of the Lord will come as a thief in the night; in the which the heavens shall pass away with a great noise, and the elements shall melt with fervent heat, the earth also and **the works that are therein shall be burned up**. (2 Peter 3:7 10)*

Every man's works will be tried by fire, but "he shall be saved - by fire,"

*[13] **Every man's work** shall be made manifest: for the day shall declare it, because it **shall be revealed by fire**; and the **fire shall try every man's work** of what sort it is. [14] If any man's work abide which he hath built thereupon, he shall receive a reward. [15] **If any man's work shall be burned, he shall suffer loss: but he himself shall be saved; yet so as by fire**. (1 Corinthians 3:13-15)*

What man usually construes as punishment from God is actually correction and beneficial to man for righteousness;

*Now **no chastening for the present seemeth to be joyous, but grievous**: nevertheless afterward it yieldeth the peaceable fruit of **righteousness** unto them which are exercised thereby. (Hebrews 12:11)*

God's will is that all men will be saved, that none shall perish, and all will come to the knowledge of the truth. Every knee will bow to Him, not forcibly but by choice. It's only man's fallible thinking that believes God will not do all that He has purposed to do. His word will not return void from what He desires and has proclaimed.

*[3] For this is good and acceptable in the sight of God our Saviour; [4] **Who will have all men to be saved**, and to come unto the knowledge of the truth. (1 Timothy 2:3-4)*

*I have sworn by myself, the word is gone out of my mouth in righteousness, and shall not return, That unto me **every knee shall bow**, every tongue shall swear. (Isaiah 45:23)*

*So shall my word be that goeth forth out of my mouth: **it shall not return unto me void, but it shall accomplish that which I please**, and it shall prosper in the thing whereto I sent it. (Isaiah 55:11)*

*While I was with them in the world, I kept them in thy name: those that thou gavest me I have kept, and **none of them is lost**, but the son of perdition; that the scripture might be fulfilled. (John 17:12)*

There are those who will argue that the word "all" doesn't really mean "all" or everyone as in "all men to be saved."

*Who will have **all men to be saved**,…(1 Timothy 2:4)*

However, they have to unequivocally agree that "death passed upon *all* men" because of sin.

*Wherefore, as by one man sin entered into the world, and death by sin; and so **death passed upon all men**, for that all have sinned: (Romans 5:12)*

The same Greek word for "all" is used in both of these verses and means "everyone."

All: G3956, *pas*: all, any, every, the whole, everyone.

After the thousand year reign.

After the reign of Christ on the earth and following the great white throne judgment, John saw the holy city, new Jerusalem coming down from God out of heaven.

*[1] And I saw a **new heaven and a new earth**: for the first heaven and the first earth were passed away; and there was no more sea. [2] **And I John saw the holy city, new Jerusalem, coming down from God out of heaven**, prepared as a bride adorned for her husband. (Revelation 21:1-2)*

*And he carried me away in the spirit to a great and high mountain, and **shewed me that great city, the holy Jerusalem, descending out of heaven from God**, (Revelation 21:10)*

Earlier, we examined the following verses where Jesus made no mention that He was preparing a place for His believers in heaven. The stronger suggestion is that He has been preparing the "holy city, new Jerusalem."

[2] In my Father's house are many mansions: if it were not so, I would have told you. I go to prepare a place for you. [3] And if I go and prepare a place for you, I will come again, and receive you unto myself; that where I am, there ye may be also. (John 14:2-3)

Scripture records that at the end of the ages all enemies are defeated and the final enemy, "death" is destroyed; the death of death. Christ, who has been reigning subjects Himself to the Father. God becomes "*all in all.*"

*[24] Then cometh the end, when he shall have delivered up the kingdom to God, even the Father; when he shall have put down all rule and all authority and power. [25] For **he must reign, till he hath put all enemies under his feet**. [26] **The last enemy that shall be destroyed is death**. [27] For he hath put all things under his feet. But when he saith all things are put under him, it is manifest that he is excepted, which did put all things under him. [28] And when all things shall be subdued unto him, **then shall the Son also himself be subject unto him that put all things under him, that God may be all in all**. (1 Corinthians 15:24-28)*

God is going to completely fulfill and restore His creation and reconcile His family back to Himself.

What does God have planned for those who love Him?

The magnificent promise from Scripture is that we are called to be heirs of God and joint-heirs with Christ in His kingdom and glory. We can only imagine how astonishing all of this can be. We will have an inheritance in all of creation.

> *[9] But as it is written,* **Eye hath not seen, nor ear heard, neither have entered into the heart of man, the things which God hath prepared for them that love him.** *[10] But God hath revealed them unto us by his Spirit: for the Spirit searcheth all things, yea, the deep things of God. (1 Corinthians 2:9-10)*

> *And if ye be Christ's, then are ye Abraham's seed, and* **heirs according to the promise.** *(Galatians 3:29)*

> *That ye would walk worthy of God,* **who hath called you unto his kingdom and glory.** *(I Thessalonians 2:12)*

> *And if children, then heirs;* **heirs of God,** *and* **joint-heirs with Christ;** *if so be that we suffer with him,* **that we may be also glorified together.** *(Romans 8:17)*

While Scripture doesn't record a single verse that says we go to heaven <u>ever</u>, we won't deny the possibility that as heirs of God and joint-heirs with Christ in creation, we could have access to it, whatever it may then be.

Summary.

- Those not included in the *first resurrection* will be raised at some time for judgment;
- They will stand before God;
- The books will be opened;
- Everyone will be judged according to their works;
- Whosoever is not found in the book of life will be cast into the lake of fire;
- The lake of fire is to burn, consume, and purify all sin and iniquity;
- Burning fire does not torture or annihilate man, it saves him;
- God's will is that all men will be saved and none perish;
- There is a future life for all men in righteousness after judgment;
- Those in Christ will be heirs in His kingdom and glory;
- We will be heirs of God and joint-heirs with Christ in all of creation;
- At the end of the ages, the Son subjects Himself to the Father;
- God will be *all in all.*

~ EIGHT ~

We bought the big lie!

When man chose to reject God in the Garden of Eden, he bought the "*BIG LIE*" by believing the enemy instead of God. This lie charted a course for all mankind, steering us to this very day.

God said:

> But of the tree of the knowledge of good and evil, thou shalt not eat of it: for in the day that thou eatest thereof **thou shalt surely die**. *(Genesis 2:17)*

The enemy said:

> *[4] And the serpent said unto the woman,* **Ye shall not surely die***:* *[5]… **ye shall be as gods,** knowing good and evil. (Genesis 3:4-5)*

Man was created mortal.

Nowhere in the whole of Scriptures is found where at first, man "*the living soul*" or any of the creatures had a promise of immortality,

99

WHAT HAPPENS WHEN WE DIE?

eternal life. All were created as "*mortal*" but Adam and Eve could eat from the tree of life in the Garden of Eden to sustain their lives. When they were cast out of the Garden, it was no longer available to them so they would die.

The *BIG LIE* deceived man into believing:

- He can naturally live forever (*be immortal and not subject to death*) apart from God and;
- He could be his own god, to decide good and evil (*right and wrong*) in his own eyes (*by his own heart, intellect and reasoning*).

Based on these deadly errors, it is now understandable why fallen man wants to believe he has a spirit (*life*) and it belongs to him and not to God. From that time to now, man has falsely believed the lie that he is immortal and cannot fully and completely perish and die.

Man does not believe and trust God.

We can see from the Scriptures:

- Man did not believe and therefore did not trust God at the beginning;
- Man has not believed and therefore has not trusted God since then;
- Man does not believe and therefore does not trust God now;
- Man did believe and therefore has trusted the lies of the enemy.

Because mortal man rejected God and His words, he became forever doomed, destined, and condemned to:

- Invalidate, annul, abolish and nullify God's simple words of truth: "*Thou shalt surely die;*"

100

- Invent, devise, concoct and conceive any doctrine, no matter how convoluted, extreme, complicated or elaborate to prove the enemy's lie, "*Ye shalt not surely die;*"
- Corrupt, alter, and distort everything of God;
- Turn the truth of God into a lie.

ANY DOCTRINE that teaches that man does not completely perish and die but somehow remains alive in a conscious state, whether in heaven, hell, or <u>any</u> other place nullifies and makes void the words of God. Reincarnation, purgatory, and all other such doctrines fall into this category.

The representation that our bodies die but our soul lives on is not at all the view of Scripture. *Souls are mortal!*

The *god-man.*

Man also believes he shall "be as gods" or simply, he can be his own god. A god can make any rule, edict, decree, law or doctrine that he desires. After all, *he is now god.*

As the *god-man* begins to create his own kingdom, he might decide that he likes seven of *The Ten Commandments;* the other three he often breaks, so he'll just toss those out. He might like the Native American's respect for the land so he'll incorporate that; he might like the serenity of Buddhism, so he'll include it too. Soon the *god-man* has finished his creation; his very own kingdom. It's different from God's, but it's exactly how he likes and wants it. It suits him just fine, and *it is good,* in his own eyes, that is.

> ***Every way of a man is right in his own eyes:*** *but the LORD pondereth the hearts. (Proverbs 21:2)*

The *god-man* has three essential laws by which he lives and governs:

- Look good;
- Be right;
- Get my way.

The only time he will waver from his laws is when it's convenient, he lusts for something, he figures out a better way to be godlier, or he sees and learns from another god who has a better mastery of godhood. This *"expression"* of spirit is antichrist spirit.

Antichrist.

In Scripture, we never find the term *"The"* Antichrist. The 1st, 2nd and 3rd books of John tells us there are many antichrists, and they were already in the world in his time.

> *[18] Little children, it is the last time: and as ye have heard that **antichrist shall come, even now are there many antichrists**; whereby we know that it is the last time. [22] Who is a liar but he that denieth that Jesus is the Christ? **He is antichrist, that denieth the Father and the Son**. (1 John 2:18, 22)*

> *For many deceivers are entered into the world, who confess not that Jesus Christ is come in the flesh. **This is a deceiver and an antichrist**. (2 John 1:7)*

The pattern we find in Scripture is that the natural comes first and then the spiritual. The temple of God in the natural was a building. The temple of God in the spiritual is man. We are the spiritual temple of God and His Spirit dwells in us.

*Howbeit that was **not first which is spiritual, but** that which is* ***natural**; and afterward that which is spiritual. (1 Corinthians 15:46)*

*Know ye not that **ye are the temple of God**, and that the Spirit of God dwelleth in you? (1 Corinthians 3:16)*

The spiritual implication is that each of us is "Antichrist", sitting in the temple of God and proclaiming that we are God. Eventually, everyone of us will have to surrender our rebellion and the throne of our hearts to the rightful owner and king, Jesus Christ.

*[4] **Who opposeth and exalteth himself above all that is called God, or that is worshipped; so that he as God sitteth in the temple of God, shewing himself that he is God**. (2 Thessalonians 2:4)*

*[19] What? know ye not that **your body is the temple of the Holy Ghost** which is in you, which ye have of God, and **ye are not your own**? [20] For **ye are bought with a price**: therefore **glorify God in your body, and in your spirit, which are God's**. (1 Corinthians 6:19-20)*

*For it is written, As I live, saith the Lord, **every knee shall bow to me**, and every tongue shall confess to God. (Romans 14:11)*

Don't expect our surrender and abdication of the throne of our heart to always be easy, pleasant, or comfortable.

Being deceived is the given.

Fallen man does not understand the gravity of his situation and condition. He always operates backward and opposite from God's ways. In man's delusions, he believes:

- He already knows the truth (*because gods don't make mistakes*) – and error (*being wrong*) keeps challenging his beliefs;
- Instead, man's beliefs are in error – and he doesn't believe the truth is waiting for him;
- Man can't comprehend the truth – until he is willing to believe he can be wrong;
- He can't believe he can be wrong – until he humbles himself before God and asks to be shown where he is being deceived;
- Man does not comprehend that being deceived is the given – because we are under the curse that happened at the beginning with the first man in the Garden of Eden.

This deception can also be compared to the condemnation of man. Jesus did not come to condemn man as many falsely believe. Man is already under condemnation (*condemned already*) from the beginning. Jesus came to save man from the condemnation. But man must believe that Jesus came to save him or he continues to remain condemned.

> [17] For **God sent not his Son into the world to condemn the world**; *but that* **the world through him might be saved**. [18] **He that believeth on him is not condemned**: *but he that* **believeth not is condemned already, because he hath not believed** *in the name of the only begotten Son of God.* (John 3:17-18)

If man refuses to receive the truth, God will:

- Send him strong delusion that he should believe a lie;

> [10] *And with all deceivableness of unrighteousness in them that perish;* **because they received not the love of the truth**, *that they might be saved.* [11] *And for this cause* **God shall send them strong delusion, that they should believe a lie:** *(2 Thessalonians 10-11)*

104

- Reject him and forget his children;

My people are destroyed for lack of knowledge: because thou hast rejected knowledge, I will also reject thee, that thou shalt be no priest to me: seeing thou hast forgotten the law of thy God, I will also forget thy children. (Hosea 4:6)

- Use foolish and weak things to confound him;

But God hath chosen the foolish things of the world to confound the wise; and God hath chosen the weak things of the world to confound the things which are mighty; (1 Corinthians 1:27)

- Not allow him to know and understand;

They know not, neither will they understand; they walk on in darkness: all the foundations of the earth are out of course. (Psalms 82:5)

- Let him learn but never able to have knowledge of the truth.

Ever learning, and never able to come to the knowledge of the truth. (2 Timothy 3:7)

How to break the cycle.

We have the promise of breaking the vicious cycle of the curse through God's unconditional love for us:

For God so loved the world, that he gave his only begotten Son, that whosoever believeth in him should not perish, but have everlasting life. (John 3:16)

Scripture is clear that the truth brings freedom but lies bring bondage to man. Man disobeys God and brings hardship upon himself, to know good and evil. But what was intended for evil God can make good. He has provided a way for us to escape the curse by turning back to Him.

We have to stop believing that we are God and quit making Him in our image, and realize that He is God and that we are made in His image.

Summary.

- Man did not trust God that *he would surely die*;
- Man trusted the enemy that *he would not surely die*;
- Man became doomed, destined, and condemned to reject God and invent false doctrines that prove the lie of the enemy;
- Almost all of man's false doctrines are based on the lie that he will not perish and die;
- Man believes that he can be his own god;
- Man sits in the temple of God proclaiming he is God;
- Man must surrender the throne of his heart to the king and rightful owner, Jesus Christ;
- Being deceived is the given;
- God will allow us to believe the lies we choose;
- Our only hope from the condemnation and the curse is Jesus Christ.

~ NINE ~

Where did we come from …
why are we here?

In this chapter we are going to answer our final question, "Why am I here?" Why were we created and what are we doing here now?

Why did God create us?

In Scripture, we can see that God created us:

- In His image and likeness;
- For dominion over all the earth;
- Predestined us unto the adoption of children by Jesus Christ;
- According to the good pleasure of His will;
- To gather together in one, all things in Christ;
- To fulfill the pleasure of His goodness;
- That the name of the Lord Jesus Christ might be glorified in us and us in Him;
- To give us the kingdom;
- To be children of God, to be sons;

- To crown us with glory and honor;
- To have dominion over the works of His hands;
- To put all things under our feet;
- For His kingdom and glory;
- To be priests of God and Christ;
- To be kings and priests;
- To reign on the earth;
- To be heirs of God and joint-heirs with Christ in His kingdom and glory;
- To judge the world;
- To judge angels;
- And more.

*[26] And **God said, Let us make man in our image, after our likeness:** and let them have dominion over the fish of the sea, and over the fowl of the air, and over the cattle, and over all the earth, and over every creeping thing that creepeth upon the earth. [27] So **God created man in his own image, in the image of God created he him; male and female created he them**. (Genesis 1:26-27)*

*For it is God which worketh in you both to will and **to do of his good pleasure**. (Philippians 2:13)*

*Having predestinated us unto the adoption of children by Jesus Christ to himself, **according to the good pleasure of his will**, (Ephesians 1:5)*

*[9] Having made known unto us **the mystery of his will, according to his good pleasure which he hath purposed in himself**: [10] That in the dispensation of the fulness of times he might gather together in one all things in Christ, both which are in heaven, and which are on*

earth; even in him: [11] In whom also we have obtained an inheritance, being predestinated according to the purpose of him who worketh all things after the counsel of his own will: (Ephesians 1:9-11)

[11] Wherefore also we pray always for you, that our God would count you worthy of this calling, and **fulfil all the good pleasure of his goodness, and the work of faith with power: [12] That the name of our Lord Jesus Christ may be glorified in you, and ye in him, according to the grace of our God and the Lord Jesus Christ.** *(2 Thessalonians 1:11-12)*

Fear not, little flock; for **it is your Father's good pleasure to give you the kingdom.** *(Luke 12:32)*

That ye would walk worthy of God, **who hath called you unto his kingdom and glory.** *(I Thessalonians 2:12)*

[16] The Spirit itself beareth witness with our spirit, that we are the children of God: [17] And if children, then **heirs; heirs of God, and joint-heirs with Christ;** *if so be that we suffer with him, that* **we may be also glorified together.** *(Romans 8:16-17)*

God is still creating man in His image and likeness, to be kings and priests and reign on the earth, and to be heirs of God and joint-heirs with Christ in His kingdom and glory. He is guiding man's maturity to prepare Him as sons for this highly esteemed position and authority. Creation is earnestly waiting too.

[19] For the earnest expectation of the creature **waiteth for the manifestation of the sons of God.** *[22] For we know that* **the whole creation groaneth and travaileth in pain** *together until now.* (Romans 8:19, 22)

What are we doing now?

We must certainly consider that we are being trained and prepared for the promised kingdom and glory that is to come. We could say that: *We are in training for the reigning!*

When man chose to disobey God and believe the lie of the enemy, he charted a course for all mankind "to know good and evil" (*right and wrong*).

Consider that since man's expulsion from the Garden of Eden, he has been living out every imaginable, mortal-human experience to have a knowledge of both good and evil. If our minds can conceive it, man has either done it or will do it, both the good and the evil. We are each fulfilling the role God has uniquely created for us to experience. Our lives are a microcosm of the macrocosm. We experience the essence of both sides of the greater experience; love and hate, loyalty and betrayal, joy and grief, forgiveness and revenge, etc.

There is no escaping our destiny. Imagine a day when we can fully see and understand that our lives were fulfilling God's greater purpose in His creation. When we realize this, we just might stop judging the experience of others. We are instructed not to judge or condemn anyone but to forgive.

> ***Judge not**, and ye shall not be judged: **condemn not**, and ye shall not be condemned: **forgive**, and ye shall be forgiven: (Luke 6:37)*

> *"There but for the grace of God go I."*
> (John Bradford, English Reformer 1510-1555)

However, we are also instructed to "judge righteous judgment" or judge behaviors according to God's divine law. For example, if we see someone stealing we can remember that it is wrong to steal and judge that behavior as unrighteous and wrong in God's eyes. Nobody gets a free pass to break His laws and if we do, we will reap the consequences of our behaviors.

*Judge not according to the appearance, but **judge righteous judgment**. (John 7:24)*

Thou shalt not steal. (Exodus 20:15)

*Be not deceived; God is not mocked: for **whatsoever a man soweth, that shall he also reap**. (Galatians 6:7)*

All the experiences will bear witness that man without God can never be. God's way will be revealed as the "only way." With any human experience left undone, God's plan could be called into question by anyone claiming that a "different way" apart from God "might somehow" have succeeded. But mortal man's way, apart and absent from God, no matter how lofty or benevolent the cause has always ended in corruption and failure.

*And **the LORD God said, Behold, the man is become as one of us, to know good and evil** ... (Genesis 3:22)*

*The **LORD hath made all things for himself**: yea, even the wicked for the day of evil. (Proverbs 16:4)*

*The **lot is cast into the lap; but the whole disposing thereof is of the LORD**. (Proverbs 16:33)*

*There is a **way which seemeth right unto a man**, but the end thereof are the ways of death. (Proverbs 14:12, 16:25)*

God knows the exact circumstances to allow into anyone's life so they will bow a knee and be saved, but Jesus said that prophecy is being fulfilled.

> *[13] Therefore speak I to them in parables: because they seeing see not; and hearing they hear not, neither do they understand. [14] And* ***in them is fulfilled the prophecy of Esaias*** *which saith, By hearing ye shall hear, and shall not understand; and seeing ye shall see, and shall not perceive: [15] For this people's heart is waxed gross, and their ears are dull of hearing, and their eyes they have closed;* ***lest at any time they should see with their eyes, and hear with their ears, and should understand with their heart, and should be converted,*** *and I should heal them. (Matthew 13:13-15)*

The great paradox.

Concerning choices and what we like to call our "free-will" to make them, consider that God is directing everything throughout His creation. The only choice we can ever make is the one that we ultimately choose. We can desire to go back and do an experience over again without our mistakes, but it was mistakes that brought us to where we are in our growth and maturity. There are no "do-overs." We can't step into the same river twice; take a step in, step out and step back in again, and the river has changed.

- Good judgment comes from wisdom;
- Wisdom comes from bad judgment.

No matter how much we want to believe that we are the master of our fate and the captain of our soul, we aren't and we never have been. God has a grand plan and whether or not it is always clear to us, His plan is unfolding precisely as it should.

*To every thing there is a season, and **a time to every purpose under the heaven**: (Ecclesiastes 3:1)*

*For I know the thoughts that I think toward you, saith the LORD, **thoughts of peace, and not of evil**, to give you an expected end. (Jeremiah 29:11)*

*[10] … My counsel shall stand, and **I will do all my pleasure**: [11] … **I have spoken it, I will also bring it to pass; I have purposed it, I will also do it**. (Isaiah 46:10-11)*

Summary.

- God created man in His image;
- We are to be priests of God and Christ and reign on the earth;
- We are in *training for the reigning*;
- God has created man to be highly esteemed;
- Man is walking out every mortal, human experience to learn good and evil;
- We will be heirs of God and joint-heirs with Christ in His kingdom and glory;
- God has a wonderful, perfect plan for us;
- God will do all His pleasure, will bring to pass what He has spoken, and do all He has purposed.

~ TEN ~

God's holy spirit and evil spirits

We previously reviewed man's spirit which is the breath of life from God and the expression or reflection of the inner self. Mortal man is destined to perish and die, but God's Holy Spirit seeks glorification by manifesting within the life and expression of man. Evil spirits also desire to express themselves in the same way. We will examine both.

God's Spirit can give man a new heart and put a new life (*spirit*) within him. Notice that the new "spirit" God puts into man is <u>His Spirit</u> and can change everything about man: the way he thinks, the way he feels and the things he does to walk in God's ways. God's Spirit now manifests in man to replace natural man's sense (*soul*), earthy, fleshy self.

> [26] ***A new heart*** *also will I give you, and **a new spirit will I put within you**: and I will take away the stony heart out of your flesh, and I will give you an heart of flesh. [27]* ***And I will put my spirit within***

you, and cause you to walk in my statutes, and ye shall keep my judgments, and do them. (Ezekiel 36:26-27)

God's Holy Spirit, the *Spirit of the Lord* or the *Spirit of God* is "life" and "power" and can refer to God's nature that is received and manifested when a person is born again by the Spirit and becomes a new creation. It also is the very nature, presence, and expression of God's power actively working in His Creation and His people. God's power, His Spirit, and presence are everywhere no matter where we go.

> *Now unto him that is able to do exceeding abundantly above all that we ask or think, **according to the power that worketh in us** (Ephesians 3:20)*

> *[7] **Whither shall I go from thy spirit? or whither shall I flee from thy presence?** [8] If I ascend up into heaven, **thou art there**: if I make my bed in hell, behold, **thou art there**. [9] If I take the wings of the morning, and dwell in the uttermost parts of the sea; [10] **Even there shall thy hand lead me**, and thy right hand shall hold me. (Psalms 139:7-10)*

The *"Spirit of God"* can grant marvelous attributes to man such as wisdom, understanding, knowledge, and so on, but these spiritual attributes come only from God and are not manifested by "the spirit of the world" or man's own intellect and reason.

> *And I have filled him with the **spirit of God**, in **wisdom**, and in **understanding**, and in **knowledge**, and in **all manner of workmanship**, (Exodus 31:3)*

> *[12] **Now we have received, not the spirit of the world, but the spirit which is of God**; that we might know the things that are freely*

*given to us of God. [13] Which things also we speak, **not in the words which man's wisdom teacheth, but which the Holy Ghost teacheth**; comparing spiritual things with spiritual. (1 Corinthians 2:12-13)*

*The thief cometh not, but for to steal, and to kill, and to destroy: **I am come that they might have life, and** that they might **have it more abundantly**. (John 10:10)*

Natural man struggles against the Spirit.

Natural man's nature is in rebellion and at war against God's Spirit, and the Spirit is against the flesh. Man must learn to crucify and die to his flesh. He must decrease so that God's Holy Spirit can be increasingly manifested within him. This struggle can be compared to two fiercely fighting dogs; a good or righteous dog and a bad or evil dog. Which dog will ultimately win? The victor will be the one that we feed.

*[17] For the **flesh lusteth against the Spirit, and the Spirit against the flesh**: and **these are contrary the one to the other**: so that ye cannot do the things that ye would. [18] But if ye be led of the Spirit, ye are not under the law. [19] Now **the works of the flesh are manifest, which are these; Adultery, fornication, uncleanness, lasciviousness, [20] Idolatry, witchcraft, hatred, variance, emulations, wrath, strife, seditions, heresies, [21] Envyings, murders, drunkenness, revellings, and such like**: of the which I tell you before, as I have also told you in time past, that they which do such things shall not inherit the kingdom of God. (Galatians 5:17-21)*

*[7] Because **the carnal mind is enmity against God**: for it is not subject to the law of God, neither indeed can be. [8] So then **they that are in the flesh cannot please God**. (Romans 8:7-8)*

*[22] But **the fruit of the Spirit is love, joy, peace, longsuffer-***

*ing, gentleness, goodness, faith, [23] **Meekness, temperance**: against such there is no law. [24] And they that are Christ's have crucified the flesh with the affections and lusts. (Galatians 5:22-24)*

> Lusteth: G1937, *epithumeo*: to set the heart upon, long for, covet, desire.
> Crucified: G4717, *stauroo*: to extinguish (subdue) passion or selfishness.

He must increase, *but I must decrease. (John 3:30)*

*[15] Love not the world, neither the things that are in the world. If any man love the world, the love of the Father is not in him. [16] For **all that is in the world, the lust of the flesh, and the lust of the eyes, and the pride of life, is not of the Father, but is of the world.** [17] And the world passeth away, and the lust thereof: but he that doeth the will of God abideth for ever. (1 John 2:15-17)*

*But **he that is joined unto the Lord is one spirit**. (1 Corinthians 6:17)*

Evil Spirits.

Devils or demons are evil spirits but are different from the fallen angels. Devils desire to manifest themselves in man and other life forms. Scripture records numerous instances of Jesus casting these unclean spirits out of afflicted people. He gave this same power to His disciples.

*[30] And Jesus asked him, saying, What is thy name? And he said, Legion: because **many devils were entered into him**. [31] And **they besought him that he would not command them to go out into the deep**. [32] And there was there an herd of many swine feeding on the mountain: and they besought him that he would suffer them to enter into them. And he suffered them. [33] **Then went the devils out of the man, and entered into the swine**: and the herd ran violently down a steep place into the lake, and were choked. (Luke 8:30-33)*

And when he had called unto him his twelve disciples, **he gave them power against unclean spirits, to cast them out,** *and to heal all manner of sickness and all manner of disease. (Matthew 10:1)*

[14] And he ordained twelve, that they should be with him, and that he might send them forth to preach, [15] And **to have power** *to heal sicknesses, and* **to cast out devils***: (Mark 3:14-15)*

Evil from Hollywood.

We can probably agree that we shouldn't get our spiritual doctrines from Hollywood movies. Hollywood steeps its films in witchcraft and idolatry. Further evidence is how they cleverly embed the number *"666"* in most, if not all of their movies today. Even the name "Hollywood" derives from a witch's wand made from the wood of holly.

Here is wisdom. **Let him that hath understanding count the number of the beast***: for it is the number of a man; and his number is* **Six hundred threescore and six***. (Revelation 13:18)*

The 1970s graphic horror movie *"The Exorcist"* showed an evil spirit (*devil*) manifesting within a young girl named Regan. Many who saw the movie often vividly recall the "green pea soup" scene where the devil spews vomit all over the priest, but do they recall how this manifestation of the evil spirit first began with Regan?

Early in the movie, we find Regan appearing to dabble innocently with a Ouija Board she had found. Without understanding the full impact of her actions, she had unwittingly tendered an invitation to a devil whom she called "Captain Howdy." She established a dialogue by merely communicating with him and opened herself to demonic influence.

Demonic influence can happen anytime we choose to disregard and disobey the instructions God has provided for our protection. We can open doors for evil spirits to claim they have a right in the affairs of our lives.

"Divination" is the practice of seeking knowledge of the future or the unknown by supernatural, occult means. It is not harmless entertainment and we should avoid any practice related to it such as astrology, fortune-telling, tarot cards, witchcraft, and necromancy.

Man has always wanted to know what the future has in store for him. We are not called to know the future beyond what God has given us but to walk in faith, trusting in God the Father and our Lord Jesus Christ.

> *And Jesus answering saith unto them,* **Have faith in God***. (Mark 11:22)*

With whom are people communicating when they consult a medium to speak with the dead?

In the Old Testament when God gave the law to the Israelites, He was very specific that attempting to communicate with the dead was an abomination to Him. It's likely that the communication would be with familiar spirits or demons and not with the departed (*the dead*).

> *[9] When thou art come into the land which the LORD thy God giveth thee,* **thou shalt not learn to do after the abominations of those nations***. [10]* **There shall not be found among you** *any one that maketh his son or his daughter to pass through the fire, or that useth divination, or an observer of times, or an enchanter, or a witch, [11] Or a charmer, or a* **consulter with familiar spirits***, or a wizard,* **or a necromancer***. [12]* **For all that do these things are an abomination unto the LORD***: and because of these abominations the LORD thy God doth drive them out from before thee. [13] Thou shalt be perfect with the LORD thy God. (Deuteronomy 18:9-13)*

"Necromancer: One who attempts to communicate with the dead."

And *have no fellowship with the unfruitful works of darkness*, *but rather reprove them. (Ephesians 5:11)*

Believers have been given power over the enemy.

Scripture is clear that evil spirits exist and can have influence in our realm, especially when we have invited them into our lives whether done consciously or unconsciously. The good news is that Christ has given us power over "*all*" the power of the enemy and the spirits are subject (*under one's control or jurisdiction*) to us.

[19] Behold, **I give unto you power** *to tread on serpents and scorpions, and* **over** __**all**__ **the power of the enemy***: and nothing shall by any means hurt you. [20] Notwithstanding in this rejoice not, that* **the spirits are subject unto you***; but rather rejoice, because your names are written in heaven. (Luke 10:19-20)*

As we trust and grow in power promised by Scripture, we can begin to use and exercise this power over sickness, disease and other forms of oppression.

For **with God nothing** *shall be* **impossible***. (Luke 1:37)*

Summary.

- In Christ, man becomes a new creature (*creation*);
- God's Holy Spirit is life and power;
- The Spirit of God can give man a new heart and put a new spirit within him;
- The Spirit of God can grant wisdom, understanding, knowledge, etc. to man;

- The flesh lusts against the Spirit and the Spirit against the flesh;
- Man must decrease so God can increase;
- He that is joined unto the Lord is one Spirit;
- Evil spirits desire to manifest in man;
- We can unwittingly invite evil spirits into our life;
- Any form of divination is forbidden;
- God expressly warned us not to attempt communication with the dead;
- Believers have been given _all_ power over the enemy;
- With God nothing is impossible.

~ ELEVEN ~

Man still insists on going to heaven

Probably the single verse most commonly used to justify that the spirit belongs to man and is separate from the breath of life from God is found in Ecclesiastes. Based on the words of this one verse, proponents vigorously argue this is proof that only our body dies but "our spirit" (*consciousness*) returns alive to be with God in heaven at the time of death. This verse is taken completely out of context and is not in harmony with either surrounding verses or the rest of Scripture.

> *Then shall the dust return to the earth as it was: and **the spirit shall return unto God who gave it**. (Ecclesiastes 12:7)*

Examine this verse with the preceding and following verses in context, and you can see this passage is speaking about the approaching of death when man goes to his long home (*grave*), and the mourners go about the streets. You can compare the time of death to the severing of a cord, a bowl cracking, a pitcher being shattered with its contents completely lost, and a broken wheel at the cistern (*well*). The context does not speak about transcending death with the hope of life in heaven following death, but instead alludes to complete and dismal loss by our return to dust.

> *[1] Remember now thy Creator in the days of thy youth, while the evil days come not, nor the years draw nigh … [5] …* **because man goeth to his long home***, and the* **mourners go about the streets***: [6] Or ever the silver cord be* **loosed***, or the golden bowl be* **broken***, or the pitcher be* **broken** *at the fountain, or the wheel* **broken** *at the cistern. [7]* **Then shall the dust return to the earth as it was***: and the spirit shall return unto God who gave it. [8]* **Vanity of vanities***, saith the preacher;* **all is vanity***. (Ecclesiastes 12:1, 5-8)*

> (silver cord) Loosed: H7368, *rachaq*: to be or become far or distant, severed.
> (golden bowl and wheel) Broken: H7533, *ratsats*: to crack, break, bruise, crush.
> (pitcher) Broken: H7665 *shabar*: to break, break in pieces, to burst.
> Vanity: H1892, *hebel*: emptiness, delusion, useless, futile, fleeting.

King Solomon, credited for writing Ecclesiastes, speaks to "*vanity of vanities*" and "*all is vanity.*" He continuously points out that everything about man is vanity, meaning that it all will end with his life; his work, passions, dreams, and riches. Man accomplishes nothing in his life that continues after his death. He is not destined for heaven at the time of death but to the grave.

Man attempted to reach heaven at the Tower of Babel.

Rebellion against God continued after the great flood at the Tower of Babel in the Land of Shinar. Man again wanted to leave earth where God had placed him and ascend into heaven without seeing death. God scattered man to keep him on the earth.

*[4] And they said, Go to, **let us build us a city and a tower, whose top may reach unto heaven**; and let us make us a name, lest we be scattered abroad upon the face of the whole earth. [5] And the LORD came down to see the city and the tower, which the children of men builded. [6] And the LORD said, Behold, the people is one, and they have all one language; and this they begin to do: and now **nothing will be restrained from them, which they have imagined to do**. [7] Go to, let us go down, and there confound their language, that they may not understand one another's speech. [8] So **the LORD scattered them abroad from thence upon the face of all the earth: and they left off to build the city**. [9] Therefore is the name of it called Babel; because the LORD did there confound the language of all the earth: and from thence **did the LORD scatter them abroad upon the face of all the earth**. (Genesis 11:4-9)*

David has not ascended into heaven.

Scripture further supports that we don't go to heaven when we die with David, the Old Testament slayer of the giant Philistine warrior Goliath. David, who would later become King of Israel did not ascend into heaven when he died. He is still both dead and buried, awaiting the resurrection. Jesus said that no one has ascended to heaven but the Son of man.

*Men and brethren, let me freely speak unto you of the patriarch **David, that he is both dead and buried, and his sepulchre is with us unto this day**. (Acts 2:29)*

*For **David is not ascended into the heavens**: but he saith himself, The LORD said unto my Lord, Sit thou on my right hand, (Acts 2:34)*

*And **no man hath ascended up to heaven**, but he that came down from heaven, even **the Son of man** which is in heaven. (John 3:13)*

The death process did not change.

Nowhere does Scripture support that the death process changed when Jesus appeared on the earth. What did change is through Him and His all-sufficient sacrifice for us on the cross, we now have the promise and hope of life everlasting (*immortality*). We can now place our emphasis, not on going to heaven when we die, but on His promise that He will resurrect us from the dead. His promise is our great hope of salvation.

> *Verily, verily, I say unto you,* **He that believeth on me hath everlasting life**. (John 6:47)

> **No man can come to me, except the Father** *which hath sent me draw him: and* **I will raise him up at the last day**. (John 6:44)

> Draw: G1670, *helkuo*: to drag, (literally or figuratively).

It's interesting to note that rebellious, stiff-necked, and disobedient man is "dragged" by the Father to the throne of grace. That's how stubborn we all can be.

Ascending into heaven is a Luciferian doctrine.

Ascending into heaven alive as immortal, without dying and a resurrection is a Luciferian doctrine from ancient times. The rebellious man still wants to be like the most High (*be his own god to decide good and evil in his own eyes*) and ascend into heaven (*as alive and without dying, instead of putting on immortality at the resurrection*).

> *[12] How art thou fallen from heaven, O Lucifer, son of the morning! how art thou cut down to the ground, which didst weaken the nations! [13] For thou hast said in thine heart,* **I will ascend into heaven,** *I will exalt my throne above the stars of God: I will sit also upon the*

*mount of the congregation, in the sides of the north: [14] **I will ascend above the heights of the clouds; I will be like the most High.** (Isaiah 14:12-14)*

This Luciferian doctrine has just been repackaged today with any teaching that denies we perish and die but insists we are *immortal and shall not surely die,* and will *ascend into heaven* at the time of death.

*And **no man hath ascended up to heaven,** but he that came down from heaven, even the Son of man which is in heaven. (John 3:13)*

*Verily, verily, I say unto you, **He that entereth not by the door into the sheepfold, but climbeth up some other way, the same is a thief and a robber.** (John 10:1)*

Summary.

- Man still insists on going to heaven when he dies;
- The sum of man's life is vanity;
- Man attempted to ascend to heaven when he rebelled at the Tower of Babel;
- The death process did not change when Jesus came;
- David did not ascend to heaven when he died;
- No one has ascended to heaven but the Son of man;
- To ascend into heaven alive is a repackaged Luciferian doctrine.

~ TWELVE ~

Other fables about death

In this comparatively longer chapter, I attempt to address most popular fables about death that support other false doctrines. Scripture does not support these fables.

Other fables about death are not found in Scripture.

So far, it has been proven from Scripture that when someone dies, they are dead, asleep, and unconscious in the grave until the resurrection when Jesus Christ returns. Some will say, if this is true then how do we explain other verses in the Bible that seem to teach that people's souls/spirits go directly to heaven when they die? The following passages are often used to justify these beliefs, but upon closer analysis, do they?

Soul Sleep.

"Soul Sleep" is another doctrine that has been growing in popularity by those who don't want to believe "everything" that is a part of

WHAT HAPPENS WHEN WE DIE?

man will perish and die at the time of death. They believe the body dies but the soul *doesn't actually die* and "only sleeps" after death. Critics accurately point out that "soul sleep" is not mentioned in Scripture. As we have already seen, the soul *doesn't actually sleep* but perishes and dies along with the body. The body goes to the grave, the soul to "the place of the unseen;" *sheol* in Hebrew, *hades* in Greek.

Both Jesus and the Apostle Paul referred to death as sleep. Perhaps they did so because even the simplest man can relate to someone asleep or at rest.

> *[11] These things said he: and after that he saith unto them,* **Our friend Lazarus sleepeth***; but I go, that I may awake him out of sleep. [12] Then said his disciples, Lord, if he sleep, he shall do well. [13] Howbeit* **Jesus spake of his death: but they thought that he had spoken of taking of rest in sleep.** *[14] Then said Jesus unto them plainly,* **Lazarus is dead.** *(John 11:11-14)*

> *For this cause many are weak and sickly among you, and* **many sleep***. (1 Corinthians 11:30)*

> *Behold, I shew you a mystery;* **We shall not all sleep***, but we shall all be changed, (1 Corinthians 15:51)*

To say that the soul remains alive and "only sleeps" is not in harmony with the rest of Scripture.

Did the thief on the cross go to be with Jesus in paradise on the day of crucifixion?

When Jesus was dying on the cross, there were two other men being crucified next to him. The first man without faith, mocked Jesus to prove that He was the Christ by saving himself and them. The second man by faith acknowledged his sin before making his appeal to Christ. He humbled himself and acknowledged that Jesus was the Christ by addressing Him as Lord. He then proceeded with his simple prayer of repentance. The implication is that Jesus immediately forgave him of his sins and promised him the kingdom. Some want to believe that the forgiven man went directly to heaven (*paradise*) on that very day instead of the grave to await a future resurrection.

> *[39] And one of the malefactors which were hanged railed on him, saying,* **If thou be Christ, save thyself and us***. [40] But the other answering rebuked him, saying, Dost not thou fear God, seeing thou art in the same condemnation? [41] And we indeed justly;* **for we receive the due reward of our deeds***: but this man hath done nothing amiss. (Luke 23:39-41)*

> *[42] And he said unto Jesus,* **Lord, remember me when thou comest into thy kingdom***. [43] And Jesus said unto him, Verily I say unto thee,* **To day shalt thou be with me in paradise***. (Luke 23:42-43)*

To day: G4594, *semeron*: today, this day, now.

Did Jesus mean the humble man would be with Him in paradise on this exact day of the crucifixion or at His return for the resurrection? The interpretation depends on where we place the "comma." Commas are not inspired but were added much later along with chapter and verse numbers for easy reference.

The first reported Bible in English to use chapter and verse numbers was the Geneva Bible published in 1560. Since then, almost all English Bibles have used them.

Did Jesus say, *"I say to you**, today you will be with me** in paradise"* or, *"**I say to you today,** you will be with me in paradise"* (at His return)? *The Scriptures 1998* is a version that places the comma to harmonize with other Scripture as seen here:

And Jesus said to him, 'Truly, I say to you <u>today,</u> *you shall be with Me in Paradise. (Luke 23:43- TS98)*

Also, Jesus didn't go to paradise on that very day (spoken by Jesus as *"to day"*) because He would be spending the next three days and three nights in the heart of the earth, the grave. The grave is not paradise. When Jesus was resurrected after three days, He came from the grave and not down from heaven.

For as Jonas was three days and three nights in the whale's belly; **so shall the Son of man be three days and three nights in the heart of the earth**. *(Matthew 12:40)*

From that time forth began Jesus to shew unto his disciples, how that he must go unto Jerusalem, and suffer many things of the elders and chief priests and scribes, and be killed, and **be raised again the third day**. *(Matthew 16:21)*

And that he was buried, and that **he rose again the third day** *according to the scriptures: (1 Corinthians 15:4)*

Jesus saith unto her, Touch me not; **for I am not yet ascended to my Father**: *but go to my brethren, and say unto them, I ascend unto my Father, and your Father; and to my God, and your God. (John 20:17)*

Another example where punctuation has been incorrectly placed can be found at Acts 19:12.

[11] And God wrought special miracles by the hands of Paul: [12] So that from his body were brought unto **the sick handkerchiefs or aprons,** *and the diseases departed from them, and the evil spirits went out of them. (Acts 19:11-12)*

132

In this verse, the misplaced comma completely changes the meaning to "... *diseases departed from the sick handkerchiefs or aprons ...*" The comma should have been placed after the word "**sick**" to read:

> *"So that from his body were brought unto the <u>**sick,**</u> handkerchiefs or aprons and the diseases departed from them, and the evil spirits went out of them."*

Did the Transfiguration show that Moses and Elias are already alive in heaven?

It might appear at the Transfiguration in Matthew 17 and Luke 9 that Moses and Elias were already alive in heaven because Peter, James and John saw Jesus talking with them.

> *[1] And after six days Jesus taketh Peter, James, and John his brother, and bringeth them up into an high mountain apart, [2] And was transfigured before them: and his face did shine as the sun, and his raiment was white as the light. [3] And, behold, **there appeared unto them Moses and Elias talking with him**. (Matthew 17:1-3)*

However, they did not really see Moses and Elias alive in heaven but saw only a "*VISION*" of them as recorded a few verses later. A vision is not reality but an experience of seeing in the supernatural.

> *And as they came down from the mountain, Jesus charged them, saying, **Tell the <u>vision</u> to no man**, until the Son of man be risen again from the dead. (Matthew 17:9)*

> *And when the voice was past, Jesus was found alone. And they kept it close, and **told no man** in those days any of those things which they had seen. (Luke 9:36)*

The parable of the rich man and Lazarus.

There are some who believe that the parable of the rich man and Lazarus in Luke 16 is an actual event based on Scriptural truth because it names an individual, Lazarus. They claim it is not a parable because Lazarus is mentioned specifically by name and in no other parable is anybody mentioned by name. There is absolutely no Scriptural support for this belief, and it is in opposition to what Jesus had already declared.

Jesus made it clear to His disciples that it was given to them to know the mysteries of the kingdom of heaven, but to others, He spoke in "parables." In Luke, He is found speaking several parables to the multitude of people gathered to hear Him. Based on what He has already said, He will be speaking in parables to them because the multitude isn't His disciples. He makes no indication or distinction whatsoever that He has somehow mysteriously switched from speaking in parables to Scriptural truth about the rich man and Lazarus.

*And he said, Unto you it is given to know the mysteries of the kingdom of God: but **to others in parables; that seeing they might not see, and hearing they might not understand.** (Luke 8:10)*

*[10] And the disciples came, and said unto him, **Why speakest thou unto them in parables**? [11] He answered and said unto them, Because it is given unto you to know the mysteries of the kingdom of heaven, but **to them it is not given**. (Matthew 13:10-11)*

*All these things **spake Jesus** unto the multitude **in parables**; and **without a parable <u>spake he not</u>** unto them: (Matthew 13:34)*

Parable: G3850, *parabole*: a similitude, fictitious narrative conveying a moral, comparison.

The parable is about a rich man who goes to a burning hell and a beggar, Lazarus, who goes to *"Abraham's bosom"* (falsely presumed by many to be heaven) following their deaths. In no other instance is *"Abraham's bosom"* found mentioned in Scripture; no second or third witness.

This one parable is used as the primary argument to justify the existence of an ever-burning, fiery hell of torment for sinners. Nowhere in *The New Testament* is found the use of threats about "fires of hell" or "unending torment" as a way of spreading the good news of the gospel.

Simple logic confirms that the story of the rich man and Lazarus IS A PARABLE:

- Jesus speaks Scriptural truth to His disciples because it is given to them to know the mysteries of the kingdom of heaven;
- To others, Jesus speaks in parables because it is not given to them;
- A multitude of non-disciples gathered around Jesus;
- Jesus says nothing to indicate that He will <u>not</u> be speaking in parables to the multitude of non-disciples;
- Therefore, Jesus will be speaking in parables to the multitude.

Further support for "the rich man and Lazarus" being a parable is how Jesus opens every parable in Luke with the words, *"a certain man"* or *"a certain rich man."* In Luke 16:19 below, we see that he opens the parable of the rich man and Lazarus with *"there was a certain rich man, which was clothed in purple and fine linen."*

- *And Jesus answering said, **A certain man** went down from Jerusalem to Jericho … (Luke 10:30);*
- *And he spake a parable unto them, saying, The ground of **a certain rich man** … (Luke 12:16);*
- *He spake also this parable; **A certain man** had a fig tree plant-*

ed in his vineyard … (Luke 13:6);

- *Then said he unto him, **A certain man** made a great supper, and bade many: (Luke 14:16);*
- *And he said, **A certain man** had two sons: (Luke 15:11);*
- *… There was **a certain rich man**, which had a steward … (Luke 16:1);*
- <u>***There was a certain rich man, which was clothed in purple and fine linen … (Luke 16:19);***</u>
- *… began he to speak to the people this parable; **A certain man** planted a vineyard … (Luke 20:9).*

Some want to use this parable to teach about the afterlife but parables don't always reflect reality. By definition, they are *"a fictitious narrative - for comparison"* and don't represent actual events.

For one example, in Judges 9:8-15, we read of a parable in which trees talked about anointing a new king for themselves. From such a parable, it would be a mistake to assume that Scripture teaches that trees talk or that trees anoint other trees to reign as kings over them. In the same way, we need to be careful about what truths we draw from "the rich man and Lazarus" parable.

*[8] **The trees went forth on a time to anoint a king over them;** and **they said** unto the olive tree, Reign thou over us. [9] But **the olive tree said** unto them, Should I leave my fatness, wherewith by me they honour God and man, and go to be promoted over the trees? [10] And **the trees said** to the fig tree, Come thou, and reign over us. [11] But **the fig tree said** unto them, Should I forsake my sweetness, and my good fruit, and go to be promoted over the trees? [12] Then **said the trees unto the vine**, Come thou, and reign over us. [13] And **the vine said** unto them, Should I leave my wine, which cheereth God and man, and go to be promoted over the trees? [14] **Then said all the trees** unto the bramble, Come thou, and reign over us. [15] And **the bramble said** unto the trees, If in truth ye anoint me king over you, then come and put*

your trust in my shadow: and if not, let fire come out of the bramble, and devour the cedars of Lebanon. (Judges 9:8-15)

Does Scripture say that being absent from the body is to be present with the Lord?

Although many teach that to be absent from the body is to be present with the Lord, is this actually found in Scripture?

> **We are** *confident, I say, and* **willing rather** *to be absent from the body, and to be present with the Lord. (2 Corinthians 5:8)*

> *[21] For to me to live is Christ, and to die is gain. [22] But if I live in the flesh, this is the fruit of my labour: yet what I shall choose I wot not. [23] For* **I am in a strait betwixt two, having a desire to depart, and to be with Christ; which is far better***: (Philippians 1:21-23)*

Paul did not actually say *"that to be absent from the body is to be present with the Lord"* as many teach, but instead he says that *"We are confident, and willing rather to be* [we would rather be or prefer to be] *absent from the body and present with the Lord."* Paul longed to be absent from the body and to be present with Christ, which he proclaimed is far better. The question is, would this transition take place at the moment of death or at Christ's second coming? Paul clarified that it would occur when *"mortality"* is *"swallowed up by life"* and *"death is swallowed up in victory,"* which happens during the resurrection *at Christ's second coming*.

To be present with the Lord without the resurrection is unobtainable.

*[16] For **the Lord himself shall descend from heaven** with a shout, with the voice of the archangel, and **with the trump of God:** and **the dead in Christ shall rise** first: [17] Then **we which are alive** and remain **shall be caught up** together with them in the clouds, to meet the Lord in the air: and **so shall we ever be with the Lord.** (1 Thessalonians 4:16-17)*

King Saul and the Woman (*Witch, Necromancer*) at Endor.

Some want to present the account of King Saul and the Witch at Endor as proof that people can be conjured back from the dead. We are going to see that this did not really happen at all.

God told King Saul to destroy Amalek and all that they had, not sparing anyone. Saul disobeyed God by sparing Agag, the king of the Amalekites. Because of his disobedience, God rejected Saul from being king over Israel. The prophet Samuel also left Saul and never saw him again.

*[2] Thus saith the LORD of hosts, I remember that which Amalek did to Israel, how he laid wait for him in the way, when he came up from Egypt. [3] **Now go and smite Amalek, and utterly destroy all that they have,** and **spare them not;** but slay both man and woman, infant and suckling, ox and sheep, camel and ass. (1 Samuel 15:2-3)*

*[8] And he took Agag the king of the Amalekites alive, and utterly destroyed all the people with the edge of the sword. [9] But **Saul and the people spared Agag, and the best of the sheep, and of the oxen, and of the fatlings, and the lambs, and all that was good, and would not utterly destroy them:** but every thing that was vile and refuse, that they destroyed utterly. (1 Samuel 15:8-9)*

*And Samuel said unto Saul, I will not return with thee: for thou hast rejected the word of the LORD, and **the LORD hath rejected thee from being king over Israel**. (1 Samuel 15:26)*

*And **Samuel came no more to see Saul until the day of his death:** nevertheless Samuel mourned for Saul: and the LORD repented that he had made Saul king over Israel. (1 Samuel 15:35)*

The Philistines then confront Saul, and because he is no longer hearing from God or His prophets, he seeks to consult a woman (*witch, necromancer*) who has a "familiar spirit." Saul knows this is an abomination to the LORD.

*But **the Spirit of the LORD departed from Saul**, and an evil spirit from the LORD troubled him. (1 Samuel 16:14)*

*[4] And the Philistines gathered themselves together, and came and pitched in Shunem: and Saul gathered all Israel together, and they pitched in Gilboa. [5] And when Saul saw the host of the Philistines, he was afraid, and his heart greatly trembled. [6] And **when Saul enquired of the LORD, the LORD answered him not**, neither by dreams, nor by Urim, **nor by prophets**. (1 Samuel 28:4-6)*

*Then said **Saul unto his servants, Seek me a woman that hath a familiar spirit**, that I may go to her, and enquire of her. And his servants said to him, Behold, **there is a woman that hath a familiar spirit at Endor**. (1 Samuel 28:7)*

*[10] There shall not be found among you any one that maketh his son or his daughter to pass through the fire, or **that useth divination**, or an observer of times, or an enchanter, or **a witch**, [11] Or a charmer,*

or a consulter with familiar spirits, or a wizard, or a necroman-
cer. [12] For all that do these things are an abomination unto the
***LORD**: and because of these abominations the LORD thy God doth*
drive them out from before thee. (Deuteronomy 18:10-12)

Saul knows the condition of the dead, but he consults the woman
with a "familiar spirit" in an attempt to bring Samuel "up from the
grave" and not "down from heaven."

Saul didn't actually see anything himself but had to ask the woman
what she saw. Saul only "perceived" that it was Samuel. Saul was putting his complete trust in a spirit medium, a witch, and necromancer
which is an abomination to God. The conversation was not between
Saul and Samuel but between Saul and a witch with a familiar or demonic spirit.

[8] And Saul disguised himself, and put on other raiment, and he went,
and two men with him, and they came to the woman by night: and he
said, I pray thee, divine unto me by the familiar spirit, and bring me him
*up, whom I shall name unto thee. [11] **Then said the woman, Whom***
***shall I bring up unto thee?** And he said, **Bring me up Samuel.** [14]*
*And **he said unto her, What form is he** of? And **she said, An old man***
cometh up; and he is covered with a mantle.** And **Saul perceived
***that it was Samuel**, and he stooped with his face to the ground, and*
bowed himself. (1 Samuel 28:8, 11, 14)

Were Enoch and Elijah Taken to Heaven?

Both Enoch and Elijah were translated. Many students of Scripture mistakenly believe that the word "translated" means to be taken
up alive without dying to be with God in heaven, but this would also
mean that someone becomes immortal by escaping death. We do not
find this belief supported anywhere in Scripture.

Translate: G3346, *metatithemi*: transfer, transport, exchange, change sides.

In His day, Jesus said that no man had ascended to heaven except Him. From His words, neither Enoch nor Elijah were alive in heaven but are still awaiting the promise of the resurrection.

*And **no man hath ascended up to heaven**, but he that came down from heaven, even **the Son of man** which is in heaven. (John 3:13)*

*And as **it is appointed unto men once to die**, but after this the judgment: (Hebrews 9:27)*

Enoch.

Enoch was translated by being taken away by God and he was not found.

*[22] And Enoch walked with God after he begat Methuselah three hundred years, and begat sons and daughters: [23] And **all the days of Enoch were three hundred sixty and five years**: [24] And Enoch walked with God: **and he was not; for God took him**. (Genesis 5:22-24)*

Paul said that Enoch was translated so that he should not see death and was not found. However, Enoch is listed along with Noah, Abraham, Moses, and others who "all died" in faith not having received the promise. The promise is immortality that Enoch will receive at the resurrection. Enoch will not see the second death after being resurrected when Jesus Christ returns.

*By faith **Enoch was translated that he should not see death; and was not found**, because **God had translated him**: for before his translation he had this testimony, that he pleased God. (Hebrews 11:5)*

These [Enoch is also named] ***all died in faith, not having received the promises***, *but having seen them afar off, and were persuaded of them, and embraced them, and confessed that they were strangers and pilgrims on the earth.* (Hebrews 11:13)

*[39] And **these all**, having obtained a good report through faith, **received not the promise**: [40] God having provided some better thing for us, **that they without us should not be made perfect**.* (Hebrews 11:39-40)

Blessed and holy is he that hath part in the first resurrection: on such the second death hath no power ... (Revelation 20:6)

Jacob was also by definition, translated to his place of burial in Sychem when he was "carried over" for burial. The same Greek word, "*metatithemi,*" is also used as with Enoch.

*[15] So Jacob went down into Egypt, and died, he, and our fathers, [16] And were **carried over** into **Sychem, and laid in the sepulcher** ...* (Acts 7:15-16)

God may have buried Enoch so no one could find him as He did with Moses. No one knows where Moses' sepulcher is to this day. God had shown the promised land to Moses but would not allow him to enter. God took Moses and by definition, "*translated*" him, buried him, and he was not found.

*[4] And the LORD said unto him, This is the land which I sware unto Abraham, unto Isaac, and unto Jacob, saying, I will give it unto thy seed: **I have caused thee to see it** with thine eyes, **but thou shalt not go over thither**. [5] So Moses the servant of the LORD died there in the land of Moab, according to the word of the LORD. [6] And **he buried**

142

*him in a valley in the land of Moab, over against Bethpeor: but **no man knoweth of his sepulchre unto this day**. (Deuteronomy 34:4-6)*

Another example is when Philip was caught away by the Spirit of the Lord. He was later found.

*[39] And when they were come up out of the water, **the Spirit of the Lord caught away Philip, that the eunuch saw him no more**: and he went on his way rejoicing. [40] But **Philip was found at Azotus**: and passing through he preached in all the cities, till he came to Caesarea. (Acts 8:39-40)*

It is now clear that Enoch did not translate alive to heaven. He died in faith not yet having received the promise of the resurrection.

Elijah.

Elijah went up by a whirlwind into heaven.

*[1] And it came to pass, when **the LORD would take up Elijah into heaven by a whirlwind**, that Elijah went with Elisha from Gilgal. [11] And it came to pass, as they still went on, and talked, that, behold, there appeared a chariot of fire, and horses of fire, and parted them both asunder; and **Elijah went up by a whirlwind into heaven**. (2 Kings 2:1, 11)*

There are three heavens referred to in Scripture, but only the "third heaven" and the "first heaven" are specifically named. The "second heaven" (*the expanse*) is only described.

Third Heaven – Heaven of Heavens; God's throne and paradise.

*But will God indeed dwell on the earth? behold, **the heaven and heaven of heavens** cannot contain thee; how much less this house that I have builded? (1 Kings 8:27)*

*[2] I knew a man in Christ above fourteen years ago, (whether in the body, I cannot tell; or whether out of the body, I cannot tell: God knoweth;) such an one caught up to **the third heaven**. [4] How that **he was caught up into paradise** ... (2 Corinthians 12:2, 4)*

Second Heaven – Space, sun, moon, planets, constellations, stars, etc.

*... the sun shall be darkened, and the moon shall not give her light, and the stars shall fall **from heaven** ... (Matthew 24:29)*

*For **the stars of heaven and the constellations** thereof shall not give their light: the **sun shall be darkened** in his going forth, and **the moon shall not cause her light to shine**. (Isaiah 13:10)*

First Heaven – Atmosphere, clouds, wind, air, whirlwinds, etc.

*And God said, Let the waters bring forth abundantly the moving creature that hath life, and **fowl that may fly above the earth in the open firmament of heaven**. (Genesis 1:20)*

*And he [Elias/Elijah] prayed again, and **the heaven gave rain**, and the earth brought forth her fruit. (James 5:18)*

*And I saw a new heaven and a new earth: for **the first heaven** and the first earth were passed away ... (Revelation 21:1)*

A whirlwind suggests that Elijah was taken into the first heaven where whirlwinds are found and not to the third heaven of God's throne. Scripture does not say that Elijah became immortal by this act of God. Elisha knew that Elijah was going to be taken away.

> *[3] And the sons of the prophets that were **at Bethel** came forth to Elisha, and said unto him, **Knowest thou that the LORD will take away thy master from thy head to day? And he said, Yea, I know** it; hold ye your peace. [5] And the sons of the prophets that were **at Jericho** came to Elisha, and said unto him, **Knowest thou that the LORD will take away thy master from thy head to day? And he answered, Yea, I know** it; hold ye your peace.* (2 Kings 2:3, 5)

Elijah held the high office as prophet of the Lord at that time. God had sent Elijah to the evil king Ahab and his son Ahaziah. Now God was choosing Elisha to hold the high office as prophet of the Lord. Elijah was aging and Ahaziah had died.

Elijah had been faithful and obedient to God. God would not remove (*demote*) him from his high office in sight of the people so that Elisha could fill the office. God removed Elijah in a whirlwind to another place. When Elijah was taken up, his mantle dropped from him and Elisha picked it up signifying that he had now become the prophet of the Lord.

> *He [Elisha] took up also the mantle of Elijah that fell from him …* (2 Kings 2:13)

Five years later, one of Jehoram's (King of Judah) first acts was to slay his brethren with a sword so they could not compete with him for the throne. For nearly six years, he did evil in God's sight before God smote him with disease. He died after reigning in Jerusalem eight years.

*[4] Now when **Jehoram** was risen up to the kingdom of his father, he strengthened himself, **and slew all his brethren with the sword,** and divers also of the princes of Israel. [18] And after all this **the LORD smote him … with an incurable disease.** [19] And it came to pass, … **after the end of two years** … **he died** … [20] … **he reigned** in Jerusalem **eight years** … (2 Chronicles 21:4, 18-20)*

Several years passed since the whirlwind removed Elijah. Then A LETTER COMES FROM ELIJAH! God had chosen Elijah to write a letter to the wicked king.

*[12] **And there came a writing to him from Elijah the prophet,** saying, Thus saith the LORD God of David thy father, Because thou hast not walked in the ways of Jehoshaphat thy father, nor in the ways of Asa king of Judah, [13] But hast walked in the way of the kings of Israel, and hast made Judah and the inhabitants of Jerusalem to go a whoring, like to the whoredoms of the house of Ahab, and also **hast slain thy brethren of thy father's house,** which were better than thyself: [14] Behold, with a great plague will the LORD smite thy people, and thy children, and thy wives, and all thy goods: [15] **And thou shalt have great sickness by disease of thy bowels, until thy bowels fall out by reason of the sickness day by day.** (2 Chronicles 21:12-15)*

From the wording of Elijah's letter, it is clear he wrote it sometime after the slayings because he speaks about it as past and before the disease because he speaks about it as the future. Two years after the king became diseased, he died after reigning eight years.

This letter also shows that the whirlwind took Elijah to another location. The letter was delivered by others who could also witness that he was alive somewhere on the earth. Scripture does not reveal how much longer Elijah lived.

The fable that Jesus went to hell between His death and resurrection.

The teaching that Jesus went to hell between His death and resurrection derived mostly from the man-made and created *"Apostle's
Creed"* and from our misunderstanding about the place of the dead.

Various organized churches slightly alter the wording to suit their
particular wishes. One example reads:

> *I believe in God, the Father almighty,* **creator** *of heaven and earth.
> I believe in Jesus Christ, God's only Son, our Lord, who was conceived by
> the* **Holy Spirit***, born of the Virgin Mary, suffered under Pontius Pilate,*
> **was crucified, died, and was buried; he descended to the dead***.* **On
> the third day he rose again***; he ascended into heaven, he is seated at
> the right hand of the Father, and he will come to judge the living and
> the dead.*

Another example with slight variations reads:

> *…* **Maker** *of heaven and earth … who was conceived by the* **Holy
> Ghost** *…* **he descended into hell** *…*

The word Hell is not defined in Scripture as a place of eternal, fiery
torment but most often as the place of the "unseen;" *sheol* in Hebrew
and *hades* in Greek. Grave, pit, and hell are words often used interchangeably in most translations.

> Hebrew: H7585, *sheol*: hades, the world of the dead, hell, pit;
> Greek: G86, *hades*: the unseen place, invisible realm, present dwelling
> place of departed souls, grave.

When Jesus was crucified and died, He indeed would have gone
to the place of the dead. Because Scripture says "the dead know not
anything," He was completely dead and unconscious in His grave and

would not have traveled anywhere. To say otherwise is to deny the teachings of Scripture about the condition of the dead. If we deny that He fully died – then He cannot have risen (*have been resurrected from the dead*) – and if He cannot have risen – our hope in the resurrection is vain (*useless*). To be raised from the dead to immortality is part of the great hope and promise of Scripture.

> *[13] But if there be no resurrection of the dead, then is Christ not risen: [14] And **if Christ be not risen**, then is our preaching vain, and **your faith is also vain**. (1 Corinthians 15:13-14)*

> ***I am he that liveth, and was dead***; *and, behold,* ***I am alive for evermore****, Amen; and* ***have the keys of hell and of death****. (Revelation 1:18)*

Jesus fully died as a man and was resurrected in the same manner as all who believe in Him will be.

Summary.

- Scripture does not support the doctrine that the soul does not die but only sleeps;
- The repentant man on the cross did not go to be with Jesus in paradise on the day of crucifixion;
- Peter, James and John only saw a "vision" of Moses and Elias alive in heaven at the transfiguration;
- Paul did not say that "to be absent from the body is to be present with the Lord." He only said he would rather be;
- King Saul did not actually see Samuel called up from the grave but rather perceived it from the witch with a familiar spirit;
- Enoch and Elijah were not translated to heaven as immortal;
- Jesus died and went to the grave as a mortal man.

THIRTEEN

False doctrine one –
Daniel's 70th week prophecy

If we had to identify a single, foundational doctrine upon which so many other false doctrines have been birthed, it might possibly be what has been termed *Daniel's 70th Week Prophecy*. From this single misapplication of Scripture, the enemy has birthed countless daughters who are the spin-off false doctrines that have directly and indirectly affected our understanding of Scripture. We will see that what happens when we die has also been influenced by these false doctrines. We begin with Daniel.

Daniel.

Daniel was one of the young men included in the seventy-year captivity and exile of the ancient Kingdom of Judah into Babylon. As the end of their captivity is approaching, Daniel is in prayer seeking understanding for the meanings of his visions. The angel Gabriel appears like a man to give him an understanding of the prophetic events to come that are found in Daniel 9:24-27.

[24] **Seventy weeks are determined upon thy people** *and upon thy holy city, to finish the transgression, and to make an end of sins, and to make reconciliation for iniquity, and to bring in everlasting righteousness, and to seal up the vision and prophecy, and to anoint the most Holy. [25] Know therefore and understand, that* **from the going forth of the commandment to restore and to build Jerusalem unto the Messiah the Prince shall be seven weeks, and threescore and two weeks:** *the street shall be built again, and the wall, even in troublous times. [26] And* **after threescore and two weeks shall Messiah be cut off, but not for himself:** *and the people of the prince that shall come shall destroy the city and the sanctuary; and the end thereof shall be with a flood, and unto the end of the war desolations are determined. [27] And* **he shall confirm the covenant with many for one week: and in the midst of the week he shall cause the sacrifice and the oblation to cease, and for the overspreading of abominations he shall make it desolate, even until the consummation, and that determined shall be poured upon the desolate.** *(Daniel 9:24-27)*

Gabriel's prophecy includes the appointed time for the promised Messiah and what His appearing will accomplish. Today, these verses are usually misinterpreted to represent a person known as "The Antichrist." But how did we arrive at this misunderstanding and false doctrine? What would anyone have to gain by changing the prophetic meaning of these four verses with a new interpretation?

The printing press and the Protestant Reformation.

Following the invention of the printing press around 1440, printed Bibles became more readily available to the common man who could now study the Scriptures for himself. As man's understanding of Scripture increased, he began to protest against corruption within the church. This movement was known as the Protestant Reformation.

The Papacy started gaining notoriety as the antichrist system as described in Scriptural prophecy, the beast of Revelation, the Little Horn of Daniel, and the Son of Perdition. The Jesuits were commissioned by the Pope to develop a new interpretation of Scripture, one that would counter this widespread view and deflect attention away from the Holy Roman Church and the Office of the Papacy (*Popes*).

The most popular new interpretation developed was "futurism" by Jesuit Priest Francisco Ribera. He manipulated prophecies of both Daniel and Revelation by applying them to a future end-time rather than to the unfolding events of history. "The Antichrist" would now become a single, wicked person who would arrive on the scene to rule the world for a seven-year period known as "The Great Tribulation."

This doctrine denied the Scriptural antichrist system as seated "in the temple of God, showing himself that he is God" as supported by many of the early Protestant reformers.

> *[3] ... and **that man of sin be revealed, the son of perdition; [4] Who opposeth and exalteth him-self above all that is called God, or that is worshipped; so that he as God sitteth in the temple of God, shewing himself that he is God**. (2 Thessalonians 2:3-4)*

The result has been a twisting and maligning of Scriptural prophecy and truth ever since. There is now a division among believers consisting of two very different paths of thought with vastly different conclusions and outcomes in the interpretation of Daniel's 70th Week Prophecy.

Futurism, the most popular path of thought.

This path of thought insists that the 70th week did not follow the 69th week (*seven weeks, and threescore and two weeks*) but was somehow moved (without Scriptural support) to a future time and depicts a futurist Antichrist. "The Antichrist" (not specifically found in Scripture) is to make a peace agreement (*covenant*) with Israel. From this interpretation derives a pre-tribulation rapture, a 7-year tribulation period known as "The Great Tribulation" (also not specifically found in Scripture), a rebuilt Jewish temple in Israel, *The Antichrist* breaking the 7-year peace agreement after 3-1/2 years, followed by 3-1/2 years of great tribulation, etc. Because this path of thought places prophetic events to some future time, they are still waiting to unfold.

Historicism, the least popular path of thought.

This path of thought insists that the 70th week immediately followed the 69th week or it would no longer be the 70th week but something else. It spoke to the arrival of the prophesied and expected Messiah who would fulfill the prophecies spoken in Daniel 9, specifically in verses 9:24-27. He would cause the sacrifice and oblation (*animal sacrifices*) to cease forever by the sacrifice of His life and finished work on the cross. This path of thought also believes that Scriptural prophecy did not cease until some future time but continues to fulfilled in history ever since.

The Linchpin – *Historicism* or *Futurism*?

A "*linchpin*" is a key-piece that supports and holds a structure together. Remove the linchpin and the whole structure will collapse. Daniel 9:24-27 is the *linchpin* upon which rests "*Daniel's 70th Week Prophecy*." From these four verses, the two very different paths of doctrinal thought emerge:

- *Historicism* identifies the verses as speaking about prophecy being fulfilled in history by the Messiah.
- *Futurism* identifies the verses as speaking about prophecy to be fulfilled at the appearing of "The Antichrist."

A fork in the road.

We face a fork in the road and the decision about which direction to travel. If we miss this crucial turn, everything else will hinge on our error. The only way to determine the correct path to follow is to let Scripture interpret itself.

> *... **no prophecy** of the scripture **is of** any **private interpretation**. (2 Peter 1:20)*

We are going to examine each verse found in Daniel 9:24-27. We will see that each individual verse has already been fulfilled in the past by the Messiah, and not future by *"The Antichrist."*

Daniel 9:24

When Daniel was in prayer seeking understanding for his visions, Gabriel appears to Daniel to give him skill and understanding about the prophetic events to come.

> *[21] Yea, **whiles I was speaking in prayer**, even the man Gabriel, whom I had seen in the vision at the beginning, being caused to fly swiftly, touched me about the time of the evening oblation. [22] And he informed me, and talked with me, and said, O Daniel, **I am now come forth to give thee skill and understanding**. (Daniel 9:21-22)*

> ***Seventy weeks are determined** upon thy people and upon thy holy city, to **finish the transgression**, and to **make an end of sins**, and to **make reconciliation for iniquity**, and to **bring in everlasting righteousness**, and to **seal up the vision and prophecy**, and to **anoint the most Holy**. (Daniel 9:24)*

153

Gabriel prophesied seventy weeks are determined upon the people to:

- Finish the transgression;
- Make an end of sins;
- Make reconciliation for iniquity;
- Bring in everlasting righteousness;
- Seal up the vision and prophecy;
- Anoint the most Holy.

These seventy weeks (490 days) are symbolic of years, with each day representing one year for a total of 490 years. This *day-for-a-year* principle is also elsewhere in Scripture.

> *After the number of the days in which ye searched the land, even forty days, **each day for a year**, shall ye bear your iniquities, even forty years, and ye shall know my breach of promise. (Numbers 14:34)*

> *And when thou hast accomplished them, lie again on thy right side, and thou shalt bear the iniquity of the house of Judah forty days: I have appointed thee **each day for a year**. (Ezekiel 4:6)*

To Finish the Transgression.

God's prophets had repeatedly warned the Israelites about their transgressions which would eventually lead to their captivity.

> *Yea, **all Israel have transgressed** thy law, even by departing, that they might not obey thy voice ... (Daniel 9:11)*

Gabriel revealed to Daniel that Israel's transgressions would finish or "come to the full." Jesus also confirmed these transgressions would "fill up."

And in the latter time of their kingdom, **when the transgressors are come to the full**, *a king of fierce countenance, and understanding dark sentences, shall stand up. (Daniel 8:23)*

[32] **Fill ye up then the measure** *of your fathers. [35] That* **upon you may come all the righteous blood shed upon the earth** ... *[36] Verily I say unto you,* **All these things shall come upon this generation**. *(Matthew 23:32, 35-36)*

The hour had come for them *"to finish the transgression."* Judgment was pronounced upon the people and Jerusalem. It was poured out upon that generation in AD 70 when Jerusalem was utterly destroyed.

Even though Jesus knew His way was the cross, He thought more of the sufferings that would come upon that generation "to finish the transgression." He wept because they had rejected Him.

[41] And when he was come near, **he beheld the city, and wept over it**, *(Luke 19:41)*

[36] Verily I say unto you, **All these things shall come upon this generation**. *[37] O* **Jerusalem, Jerusalem**, *thou that killest the prophets, and stonest them which are sent unto thee, how often* **would I have gathered thy children** *together, even as a hen gathereth her chickens under her wings, and* **ye would not!** *[38] Behold,* **your house is left unto you desolate**. *(Matthew 23:36-38)*

"To finish the transgression" was the betrayal, crucifixion, and murder of the promised Messiah, the Lord Jesus Christ.

To Make an End of Sins.

Jesus made an end of sins by His sacrifice on the cross:

*Who being the brightness of his glory, and the express image of his person, and upholding all things by the word of his power, when he had **by himself purged our sins**, sat down on the right hand of the Majesty on high; (Hebrews 1:3)*

*For then must he often have suffered since the foundation of the world: but now once in the end of the world hath **he appeared to put away sin by the sacrifice of himself.** (Hebrews 9:26)*

*[12] But this man, after he had offered **one sacrifice for sins for ever**, sat down on the right hand of God; [13] From henceforth expecting till his enemies be made his footstool. (Hebrews 10:12-13)*

To Make Reconciliation for Iniquity.

By the forgiveness of our sins, we can now be reconciled to God and be saved:

*[8] But God commendeth his love toward us, in that, while we were yet sinners, **Christ died for us**. [9] Much more then, being now **justified by his blood, we shall be saved** from wrath through him. [10] For if, when we were enemies, **we were reconciled to God by the death of his Son, much more, being reconciled, we shall be saved by his life.** (Romans 5:8-10)*

To Bring in Everlasting Righteousness.

Jesus Christ is the *Lord of righteousness.*

*[5] Behold, the days come, saith the LORD, that I will raise unto David a righteous Branch, and **a King shall reign and prosper, and shall execute judgment and justice in the earth.** [6] In his days Judah shall be saved, and Israel shall dwell safely: and this is his name whereby he shall be called, **THE LORD OUR RIGHTEOUSNESS**. (Jeremiah 23:5-6)*

*[21] But now the **righteousness of God without the law is manifested**, being witnessed by the law and the prophets; [22] Even the **righteousness of God** which is **by faith of Jesus Christ** unto all and upon all them that believe: for **there is no difference:** [25] Whom God hath set forth to be a propitiation through faith in his blood, to declare **his righteousness for the remission of sins** that are past, through the forbearance of God; [26] To declare, I say, at this time **his righteousness**: that he might be just, and the **justifier** of him **which believeth in Jesus**. (Romans 3:21-22, 25-26)*

To Seal Up the Vision and Prophecy.

Daniel, given prophetic vision and understanding about the events that would unfold, was told not to reveal them.

*But thou, O Daniel, **shut up the words, and seal the book**, even to the time of the end: many shall run to and fro, and knowledge shall be increased. (Daniel 12:4)*

The words of Isaiah along with those spoken by Jesus give a remarkable account of how the vision and prophecy were sealed up to cause spiritual blindness in the people and their rulers. Although they read the prophets, they could not understand. They would condemn Jesus, the Messiah. Both eye and ear would be closed so they could not see or hear.

*[9] And he said, Go, and tell this people, **Hear ye indeed, but understand not**; and **see ye indeed, but perceive not.** [10] Make the heart of this people fat, **and make their ears heavy, and shut their eyes**; lest they see with their eyes, and hear with their ears, and understand with their heart, and convert, and be healed. (Isaiah 6:9-10)*

*[11] He answered and said unto them, Because **it is given unto you** to know the mysteries of the kingdom of heaven, but **to them it is not given.** [13] Therefore speak I to them in parables: because **they seeing see not; and hearing they hear not, neither do they under-stand.** [14] And in them is **fulfilled the prophecy of Esaias**, which saith, **By hearing ye shall hear, and shall not understand; and see-ing ye shall see, and shall not perceive:** [15] For this people's heart is waxed gross, and their ears are dull of hearing, and their eyes they have closed; lest at any time they should see with their eyes, and hear with their ears, and should understand with their heart, and should be converted, and I should heal them. [16] But **blessed** are **your eyes, for they see: and your ears, for they hear.** (Matthew 13:11, 13-16)*

To Anoint the Most Holy.

The words, "*Messiah*" (in Hebrew) and "*Christ*" (in Greek) mean the same thing: "*The Anointed One.*" Jesus is the "Holy One of God", "the Messiah", "the Anointed of God", "the Christ" who was appointed and anointed to accomplish the great work of redemption. He did this by the sacrifice of Himself.

*[18] The Spirit of the Lord is upon me, because **he hath anointed me** to preach the gospel to the poor; he hath sent me to heal the brokenhearted, to preach deliverance to the captives, and recovering of sight to the blind, to set at liberty them that are bruised, [19] To preach the acceptable year of the Lord. (Luke 4:18-19)*

*How **God anointed Jesus of Nazareth** with the Holy Ghost and with power: who went about doing good, and healing all that were op-pressed of the devil; for God was with him. (Acts 10:38)*

*Thou hast loved righteousness, and hated iniquity; therefore God, even thy **God, hath anointed thee** with the oil of gladness above thy fellows. (Hebrews 1:9)*

Jesus was "anointed" at His baptism in Jordan at the close of the 69th week (483 years) and the beginning of the 70th week (the 70th – seven-year period).

*[15] And Jesus answering said unto him, Suffer it to be so now: for thus it becometh us **to fulfil all righteousness** ... [16] And Jesus, when he was baptized, went up straightway out of the water: and, lo, the heavens were opened unto him, and he saw the **Spirit of God descending like a dove, and lighting upon him**: [17] And lo a voice from heaven, saying, **This is my beloved Son, in whom I am well pleased.** (Matthew 3:15-17)*

Daniel 9:25

This verse speaks about a decree that would mark the beginning of the prophecy when the Messiah would arrive at the end of the 69th week (seven and threescore and two weeks: 7 + 62 = 69 weeks) and at the beginning of the 70th week (the 70th – seven-year period).

*Know therefore and **understand**, that **from the going forth of the commandment to restore and to build Jerusalem unto the Messiah the Prince shall be seven weeks, and threescore and two weeks**: the street shall be built again, and the wall, even in troublous times. (Daniel 9:25)*

Historians know of at least four decrees made by the Persian emperors to rebuild Jerusalem, but only one decree fits the time constraint *"until Messiah the Prince"* spoken by Gabriel. This decree was made by Artaxerxes I in 457 BC. Adding 483 years (69 weeks x 7 years = 483 years) to the decree places the time at or near the baptism of Jesus and the beginning of His ministry in AD 27.

Daniel 9:26

The Messiah will be cut off (*crucified and killed*), but it will not be for himself. It will be for all mankind.

Some want to use Daniel 9:26 alone to claim that the Messiah was cut off at the end of the 69th week instead of the middle of the 70th week. With this claim, the verses no longer harmonize. They do still harmonize when the Messiah is cut off in the middle of the 70th week.

> And after **threescore and two weeks shall Messiah be cut off, but not for himself:** and the people of the prince that shall come shall destroy the city and the sanctuary; and the end thereof shall be with a flood, and unto the end of the war **desolations are determined**. (Daniel 9:26)

The people of the prince, the Roman Army under General Titus, destroyed Jerusalem and the sanctuary (*temple*) in AD 70 and desolations (*devastations*) were determined (*to wound*).

> And Jesus said unto them, See ye not all these things? verily I say unto you, **There shall not be left here one stone upon another, that shall not be thrown down.** (Matthew 24:2)

Daniel 9:27

The Messiah shall confirm the covenant with many during the 70th week but after 3-1/2 years in the midst of the week will be His death and crucifixion in AD 31. These events will cause the sacrifice and oblation (*animal sacrifices for sin done in the temple*) to cease forever as atonement for sin.

*And **he shall confirm the covenant** with **many** for one week: and in the **midst of the week** he shall cause the **sacrifice and the oblation to cease**, and for the overspreading of abominations he shall make it desolate, even until the consummation, and **that determined shall be poured upon the desolate**. (Daniel 9:27)*

The new covenant was "confirmed" (*make firm, prevail*) with many ONLY through the shed blood and death of Jesus Christ, which occurred during the middle of the 70ᵗʰ week (3-1/2 years into the week).

*Behold, the days come, saith the LORD, that **I will make a new covenant** with the house of Israel, and with the house of Judah: (Jeremiah 31:31)*

*For this is **my blood of the new testament** [contract, covenant], which is shed for **many** for the remission of sins. (Matthew 26:28)*

*By so much was **Jesus made a surety of a better testament**. (Hebrews 7:22)*

*But now hath he obtained a more excellent ministry, by how much also **he is the mediator of a better covenant**, which was established upon better promises. (Hebrews 8:6)*

*And for this cause **he is the mediator of the new testament**, that by means of death, for the redemption of the transgressions that were under the first testament, they which are called might receive the promise of eternal inheritance. (Hebrews 9:15)*

*And to **Jesus the mediator of the new covenant**, and to the blood of sprinkling, that speaketh better things than that of Abel. (Hebrews 12:24)*

*Now the God of peace, that brought again from the dead our Lord Jesus, that great shepherd of the sheep, through the blood of the **everlasting covenant**, (Hebrews 13:20)*

*He shall see of the travail of his soul, and shall be satisfied: by his knowledge shall my righteous servant justify **many**; for he shall bear their iniquities. (Isaiah 53:11)*

*Even as the Son of man came not to be ministered unto, but to minister, and to give his life a ransom for **many**. (Matthew 20:28)*

The final fulfillment of the last 3-1/2 years of the 70th week came when Steven was falsely accused of blasphemy. After Steven had called to task the elders and scribes about their wicked and evil deeds of killing the prophets and the Messiah, they became angered and stoned him to death (Acts 7:51-60). The gospel would now go to the nations.

The evidence of Scripture speaks for itself and makes it abundantly clear that "Daniel's 70th Week Prophecy" is about the Messiah and not "The Antichrist." This misunderstanding will lead to a repackaged Luciferian doctrine with a twist that we will examine in the next chapter, "The Rapture."

Summary.

- There is no Scriptural support that "The Antichrist" will make, confirm or break a covenant with anyone, including Israel;
- There is no Scriptural support to show that the 70th week of Daniel did not follow the 69th week or was somehow moved to a future time;
- There aren't two, three, or more witnesses to support a "future" 70th week prophecy;

- There is overwhelming Scriptural support that Daniel 9:24-27 foretold the most important event in the history of man at that time; the arrival of the promised Messiah for His atoning work on the cross.

~ FOURTEEN ~

False doctrine two –
The rapture

If we had not been deceived and had properly applied "Daniel's 70th Week Prophecy," it is doubtful that our second false doctrine could have ever emerged, "The Rapture." This doctrine has added untold chaos and controversy among believers about what happens when we die. There are slight variations of this doctrine among its followers, but closer examination will show that it is still a repackaged Luciferian doctrine, but with a twist. Recall that any doctrine that proclaims we will ascend into heaven alive without dying and the need for a resurrection is false when compared with Scripture.

Earlier we learned that both the body and soul perish and die to-gether, but the Spirit or breath of life does not die and returns to God who gave it. The twist is another un-Scriptural teaching that living believers will be transported off the earth to heaven to escape "The Great Tribulation." They supposedly will return with Jesus back to the earth from heaven after the tribulation period for the resurrection of their bodies.

I admit there was a time when I subscribed to "The Pre-Tribulation Rapture." I had been taught it as a child in a small church with a loving congregation; more akin to family than just church-goers. When I was young, I never gave thought to even question it. I had not yet learned to be a good "Berean" and to search the Scriptures. When I finally did learn, false teachings like the "The Pre-Tribulation Rapture" became an affront to my senses.

The Pre-Tribulation Rapture.

Some have polluted the rightly named "first resurrection" to an event they call the "rapture of the church." The event is usually in the context of either a *pre-mid-post* tribulation period but is most often taught as "The Pre-Tribulation Rapture."

One cannot find the English word "rapture" anywhere in Scripture. Critics say that Cyrus Ingerson Scofield in his *Scofield Reference (Study) Bible* took the Latin word "*raeptius*" (*to take away*) and used it for the similar Greek word "*harpazo*" (*to catch up*). "*Harpazo*" is translated "caught up" and is used to teach that those in Christ will be *caught up* to meet the Lord in the air. Scripture does indeed support that believers will be "caught-up" but this happens at the first resurrection. It is not a separate event known as "the rapture."

Rapture enthusiasts believe they will be transported off the earth by Jesus Christ, sometime before His actual return for the resurrection. Some allege that Christ will make two, others advocate three, trips to the earth. His first trip is to supposedly rescue His followers from "The Great Tribulation." The passage most used to support this belief is:

> *[15] For this we say unto you by the word of the Lord, that we which are alive and remain unto the coming of the Lord shall not prevent [precede] them which are asleep. [16] For the Lord himself shall descend from heaven with a shout, with the voice of the archangel, and with*

the trump of God: and the dead in Christ shall rise first: [17] **Then we which are alive and remain shall be caught up** *together with them in the clouds, to meet the Lord in the air: and so shall we ever be with the Lord. (1 Thessalonians 4:15-17)*

Caught up: G726, *harpazo*: to seize, catch (away, up), pluck, pull, take.

What did Jesus say?

Jesus spoke just the opposite about being taken out of the world to escape evil.

I pray not that thou shouldest take them out of the world, *but that thou shouldest keep them from the evil. (John 17:15)*

These things I have spoken unto you, that in me ye might have peace. **In the world ye shall have tribulation: but be of good cheer; I have overcome the world**. *(John 16:33)*

When speaking about the generation when the destruction of Jerusalem and the temple would occur (in AD 70), Jesus presented an example and pattern that He comes "*after tribulation before His appearing.*" Rapture supporters insist that He will come to rescue them "*after His appearing before tribulation.*"

[29] **Immediately after the tribulation of those days** *shall the sun be darkened, and the moon shall not give her light, and the stars shall fall from heaven, and the powers of the heavens shall be shaken: [30] And* **then shall appear the sign of the Son of man in heaven**: *and then shall all the tribes of the earth mourn, and they* **shall see the Son of man coming in the clouds of heaven** *with power and great glory. [31] And he shall send his angels with a great sound of a trumpet, and* **they shall gather together his elect** *from the four winds, from one end of heaven to the other. (Matthew 24:29-31)*

> *[24] But **in those days, after that tribulation**, the sun shall be darkened, and the moon shall not give her light, [25] And the stars of heaven shall fall, and the powers that are in heaven shall be shaken. [26] And **then shall they see the Son of man coming** in the clouds with great power and glory. (Mark 13:24-26)*

> *For then shall be **great tribulation**, such as was not since the beginning of the world to this time, no, nor ever shall be. (Matthew 24:21)*

The purpose of tribulation.

We live in a lost and dying world just like Jesus said it would be in the last days. Tribulation (*pressure, affliction, anguish, burden, persecution, trouble*) serves a beneficial purpose to turn man back to "righteousness" or "*right-doing.*" Man seldom changes because he sees the light; he most often changes because he "feels the heat."

> *With my soul have I desired thee in the night; yea, with my spirit within me will I seek thee early: for **when thy judgments are in the earth, the inhabitants of the world will learn righteousness.** (Isaiah 26:9)*

> *Now no chastening for the present seemeth to be joyous, but grievous: nevertheless **afterward it yieldeth the peaceable fruit of righteousness** unto them which are exercised thereby. (Hebrews 12:11)*

What Scripture calls tribulation and great tribulation, man has gone so far as to concoct an event that he names "The Great Tribulation" and has assigned a seven year time period to it. Neither has a basis in Scripture. There is ample evidence that man has and will continue to experience untold tribulation. We only have to open our eyes to see the trouble on the horizon.

*And I said unto him, Sir, thou knowest. And he said to me, These are they which came out of **great tribulation**, and have washed their robes, and made them white in the blood of the Lamb. (Revelation 7:14)*

The beginnings.

Critics claim the rapture doctrine never existed before the 1830s. They report it began with a vision of a young Scottish girl, Mary Mac-Donald, while she was in a trance. It was picked up by the Irish-born minister and lawyer John Darby, who brought it to America sometime in the early 1860s to the late 1870s. The doctrine was later included in the *Scofield Reference (Study) Bible* that was generously handed out to pastors and ministers in the early 1900s. Cyrus Ingerson Scofield became a mentor to Lewis Sperry Chafer, who founded the current-day Dallas Theological Seminary, a major proponent for the rapture doctrine teaching. The doctrine also made its way into many other seminaries and to the established teaching of today.

God's last word to us.

In times past, God spoke to us through his prophets but His last word to us is by His Son. We are to be cautious of any new, non-Scriptural revelation or gospel of man. Paul also warned us that if someone comes teaching another Jesus, another spirit or another gospel, we are to well bear (*to hold one's self up against*) with him. It happened in Paul's day and it's also happening in our day.

*[1] God, who at sundry times [in many portions] and in divers manners [in many ways] spake in time past unto the fathers by the prophets, [2] **Hath in these last days spoken unto us by his Son**, whom he hath appointed heir of all things, by whom also he made the worlds; (Hebrews 1:1-2)*

*[6] I marvel that ye are so soon removed from him that called you into the grace of Christ unto another gospel: [7] Which is not another; but **there be some that trouble you, and would pervert the gospel of Christ**. (Galatians 1:6-7)*

*[3] But I fear, lest by any means, as the serpent beguiled Eve through his subtilty, so your minds should be corrupted from the simplicity that is in Christ. [4] **For if he that cometh preacheth another Jesus, whom we have not preached, or if ye receive another spirit, which ye have not received, or another gospel, which ye have not accepted, ye might well bear** [to hold oneself up against] **with him.** (2 Corinthians 11:3-4)*

Neither Jesus nor Paul taught "a rapture of the church of believers." When Jesus told Martha that her dead brother would rise again, Martha confirmed that she knew her brother Lazarus would rise again in the resurrection at the last day. Jesus did not correct her by saying Lazarus would first rise in a rapture that precedes the resurrection.

*[23] Jesus saith unto her, Thy brother shall rise again. [24] Martha saith unto him, **I know that he shall rise again in the resurrection at the last day**. (John 11:23-24)*

Scriptural passages most often used to justify a rapture.

The passages most often used to justify a rapture are: John 14:2-3, 1 Corinthians 15:49-55, Philippians 3:20-21, 1 Thessalonians 4:15-17, and 2 Thessalonians 2:1-7. You may recognize most of these verses as applying to the coming resurrection that we explored earlier. It takes a lot of skillful manipulation to pull a rapture out of these verses.

We earlier saw that all of these verses pertain to the coming "first resurrection."

[49] And as we have borne the image of the earthy, we shall also bear the image of the heavenly. [50] Now this I say, brethren, that flesh and blood cannot inherit the kingdom of God; neither doth corruption inherit incorruption. [51] Behold, I shew you a mystery; We shall not all sleep, but we shall all be changed, [52] In a moment, in the twinkling of an eye, at the last trump: for the trumpet shall sound, and the dead shall be raised incorruptible, and we shall be changed. [53] For this corruptible must put on incorruption, and this mortal must put on immortality. [54] So when this corruptible shall have put on incorruption, and this mortal shall have put on immortality, then shall be brought to pass the saying that is written, Death is swallowed up in victory. [55] O death, where is thy sting? O grave, where is thy victory? (1 Corinthians 15:49-55)

[20] For our conversation is in heaven; from whence also we look for the Saviour, the Lord Jesus Christ: [21] Who shall change our vile body, that it may be fashioned like unto his glorious body, according to the working whereby he is able even to subdue all things unto himself. (Philippians 3:20-21)

[15] For this we say unto you by the word of the Lord, that we which are alive and remain unto the coming of the Lord shall not prevent them which are asleep. [16] For the Lord himself shall descend from heaven with a shout, with the voice of the archangel, and with the trump of God: and the dead in Christ shall rise first: [17] Then we which are alive and remain shall be caught up together with them in the clouds, to meet the Lord in the air: and so shall we ever be with the Lord. (1 Thessalonians 4:15-17)

Subscribers to a rapture believe the "falling away" will be at the end times and won't affect them because they won't be here. A study of history shows that it was Rome and the Roman army that held back and kept in the natural, the man of sin, the son of perdition, the Papacy (*office of the Popes of Rome*) from coming to power until AD 538. The Roman Catholic Church, the Orthodox Church and the Protestant Churches subscribed to "The Nicene Creed" which began in AD 325 at the Council of Nicea. There the Roman Emperor Constantine started the religion of Christianity based on Roman pagan worship rituals and abandoned the teachings of the Holy Scriptures.

> *[1] Now we beseech you, brethren, by the coming of our Lord Jesus Christ, and by our gathering together unto him, [2] That ye be not soon shaken in mind, or be troubled, neither by spirit, nor by word, nor by letter as from us, as that the day of Christ is at hand. [3] Let no man deceive you by any means:* **for that day shall not come, except there come a falling away first***, and that man of sin be revealed, the son of perdition; [4] Who opposeth and exalteth himself above all that is called God, or that is worshipped; so that he as God sitteth in the temple of God, shewing himself that he is God. [5] Remember ye not, that, when I was yet with you, I told you these things? [6] And now ye know what withholdeth that he might be revealed in his time. [7] For the mystery of iniquity doth already work:* **only he who now letteth will let, until he be taken out of the way***. (2 Thessalonians 2:1-7)*

Left behind.

Scores of movies and videos and millions of books have been sold that teach the plight of those "left behind" on the earth to suffer wrath during *The Great Tribulation*; after rapture believers have been transported off the earth to escape the horrors. This false teaching has left an indelible imprint on those not grounded in Scripture. Based on the written word, the biggest thing "left behind" with the rapture doctrine has been the truth.

Extremely large numbers of fundamental Christians subscribe to a coming rapture. If we follow the money trail, rapture can be big business with a wide audience. Don't think for a minute that the world isn't eager to capitalize on anything and everything it can exploit.

*For **many shall come in my name**, saying, I am Christ; **and shall deceive many**. (Matthew 24:5)*

*And **many false prophets shall rise, and shall deceive many**. (Matthew 24:11)*

*For the **love of money is the root of all evil**: which while some coveted after, they have erred from the faith, and pierced themselves through with many sorrows. (1 Timothy 6:10)*

*And **have no fellowship with the unfruitful works of darkness**, but rather reprove them. (Ephesians 5:11)*

Summary.

- A "rapture" is not found anywhere in Scripture;
- "The Rapture" is a false doctrine contrived from verses that apply and speak to the "first resurrection;"
- Scripture supports one and only one return of Jesus Christ;
- Jesus Christ returns for the resurrection, not a rapture;
- Jesus Christ returns *after* tribulation, not *before*;
- Those "caught up" do not go with Jesus Christ to heaven;
- Those "caught up" return with Jesus Christ to the earth;
- They live and reign with Him a thousand years on the earth, not in heaven;
- A rapture is only found in movies, videos, books, and other man-made things that are marketed and sold.

~ FIFTEEN ~

Thoughts about time and eternity

Time and eternity.

We have often been conditioned to think of eternity in terms of a very long, long time. A portion of the song *"Amazing Grace"* also alludes to this concept by referring to time in a measurement of "ten thousand years" as "no less days" on the eternal scale.

> *When we've been there **ten thousand years***
> *Bright shining as the sun.*
> ***We've no less days** to sing God's praise*
> *Than when we've first begun.*

There are excellent Scriptural scholars who point out the often mistranslated use of the words "aionian" and "aion" *(from which we get the English words, "eonian" and "eon")*. These words are frequently mistranslated as "eternity", "eternal", "everlasting", "forever", or equivalent

WHAT HAPPENS WHEN WE DIE?

terms to mean "without end." However, there are times when these words have been translated to mean "temporal" *(temporary)* and refer to specific periods of time.

Bob Evely, in his book *"At the End of the Ages, The Abolition of Hell"* has done an exceptional job to show how these words found in Scripture cannot always mean "never-ending." One such example includes different variations:

> *Hebrews 1:8*   *"the eon of the eon"*
> *Ephesians 3:21*   *"the eon of the eons"*
> *Galatians 1:5*   *"the eons of the eons"*
> *If "eon" is eternity, what do these things mean?*

Students of Scripture would do well to exercise caution whenever they find these words in their studies rather than accepting them as incontrovertible truth without further investigation. Recall from earlier that in *"The Translators to the Reader"*, preface to the original *Kings James Version* of the Bible, the translators encouraged us

> "... that variety of Translations is profitable for the finding out of the sense of the Scriptures ..."

Man's wide-ranging theological beliefs have created a false notion that all time must end some day so eternity can begin. Scripture does not support the idea that time will ever end and reveals only that the "eons" or "ages" will draw to a close as they are replaced by the "eons" or "ages" that are to follow.

> *[6] For unto us a child is born, unto us a son is given: and the government shall be upon his shoulder: and his name shall be called Wonderful, Counsellor, The mighty God, The everlasting Father, The Prince of Peace. [7]* **Of the increase of his government and peace there**

shall be no end, *upon the throne of David, and upon his kingdom, to order it, and to establish it with judgment and with justice* **from henceforth even for ever**. *The zeal of the LORD of hosts will perform this.* (Isaiah 9:6-7)

Scripture does promise a time when death, the final enemy, will be defeated. Believers will become immortal at the resurrection, which implies that they will be alive at the end of the eon (*age*), the end of the eons (*ages*), the eons (*ages*) of the eons (*ages*), or any other time God has purposed for them.

No passing of time for the dead.

Because the dead are unconscious in the place of the unseen, there is no concept of passing time for them. It suggests they close their eyes to death only to immediately (*or what seems immediately to them*) reopen their eyes to the resurrection. They could have been dead for a thousand years but their awakening might only seem like an instant in their eyes.

I have gone unconscious a few times in my life, but each time didn't seem like I went unconscious at all because it all happened so fast. I believed I had "almost" gone unconscious but didn't quite go all the way out. In actuality, I was definitely out for several seconds to a few minutes. I was out and back in a moment, in the twinkling of an eye.

At the resurrection, both the dead and alive in Christ are changed so quickly that Scripture describes it as "a moment, in the twinkling of an eye." They are changed to become immortal, which means they will never die again. We will have immortality, just as Jesus promised.

[51] Behold, I shew you a mystery; We shall not all sleep, but **we shall all be changed**, *[52]* **In a moment, in the twinkling of an eye**, *at the last trump: for the trumpet shall sound, and the dead shall be raised*

*incorruptible, and we shall be changed. [53] For this corruptible must put on incorruption [indestructibility], and **this mortal must put on immortality**. [54] So when this corruptible shall have put on incorruption, and this mortal shall have put on immortality, then shall be brought to pass the saying that is written, **Death is swallowed up in victory**. (1 Corinthians 15:51-54)*

I am he that liveth, and was dead; and, behold, I am alive for evermore, Amen; and have the keys of hell and of death. (Revelation 1:18)

Alive when Christ returns?

There have always been those of us who dream of being alive when Christ returns for the resurrection of the believers. Scripture and our own observations make it clear that not all will be. If we give this some thought, if we are not alive when He returns it will only be for an instant anyhow.

*For the living know that they shall die: but **the dead know not any thing** … (Ecclesiastes 9:5)*

Where are we on the time scale?

God created everything in six days and rested on the seventh day.

*And God saw every thing that he had made, and, behold, it was very good. And the evening and the morning were **the sixth day**. (Genesis 1:31)*

*And **on the seventh day God ended his work** which he had made; **and he rested** on the seventh day from all his work which he had made. (Genesis 2:2)*

It is interesting to note that, according to Genesis during the period of creation, we find the phrase, "And the evening and the morning were the (*1ˢᵗ–6ᵗʰ*) day." We find no such phrase after the 7ᵗʰ day. Could this mean that the 7ᵗʰ day has no ending?

One day with the Lord is a thousand years, and a thousand years as one day.

> For **a thousand years in thy sight** *are but* **as yesterday** *when it is past, and as a watch in the night. (Psalms 90:4)*

> *But, beloved, be not ignorant of this one thing, that* **one day is with the Lord as a thousand years, and a thousand years as one day**. *(2 Peter 3:8)*

How long has man been on the earth? For thoughtful speculation ONLY.

Scripture doesn't age the earth or man but some have presented some interesting thoughts from what is written.

Because one day is equal to a thousand years, the six days of creation could be symbolic for 6,000 years for mortal man on the earth. The seventh day, a day of rest, could be symbolic of the 1,000 years following the resurrection, when Christ returns to establish His kingdom.

> *Blessed and holy is he that hath part in the first resurrection: on such the second death hath no power, but* **they shall be priests of God and of Christ, and shall reign with him a thousand years**. *(Revelation 20:6)*

> *And hast made us unto our God* **kings and priests:** *and* **we shall reign on the earth**. *(Revelation 5:10)*

God spoke the light into existence on the fourth day. Some place the birth of Jesus, the true Light, at approximately 4,000 years (4ᵗʰ day) from creation.

*[14] And God said, **Let there be lights** in the firmament of the heaven ... [19] And the evening and the morning were **the fourth day**. (Genesis 1:14, 19)*

*[4] In him was life; and **the life was the light of men**. [5] And the **light shineth in darkness; and the darkness comprehended it not**. [6] There was a man sent from God, whose name was John. [7] The same came for a witness, **to bear witness of the Light**, that all men through him might believe. [8] He was not that Light, **but was sent to bear witness of that Light**. [9] **That was the true Light, which lighteth every man that cometh into the world**. (John 1:4-9)*

Still only thoughtful speculation, but if symbolic, then 4,000 years from Jesus to today is approximately 6,000 years, or the end of the sixth day and before His return for the seventh day (1,000 years).

Summary.

- We should exercise caution in our studies whenever we encounter the words "eternity," "eternal", or other terms that mean unending;"
- Man's theological beliefs have created a false notion that time must end someday so eternity can begin;
- There is no concept of passing time for the dead;
- The dead may close their eyes to death, only to immediately reopen them to the resurrection;
- If we aren't included with those alive at the resurrection, it may only be an instant for us anyhow;
- One day with the Lord is a thousand years and a thousand years as one day.

~ SIXTEEN ~

What if scripture doesn't line up with my beliefs?

Our journey is drawing to a close and our final destination is clearly in sight. We have discovered:

- Man became a living soul at creation, and the body and soul are inseparable;
- Man became alive with the breath of life from God;
- Man is mortal: he is destined to die;
- Everything that is a part of man will perish and die;
- When man dies, the breath of life (*spirit*) returns to God who gave it;
- Man will not go anywhere as alive and conscious after he dies;
- Believers will be resurrected when Christ returns;
- Believers will put on incorruption and immortality at the resurrection;
- Believers will live and reign with Christ on the earth for a thousand years;

- Others will be resurrected at some time to stand before God for judgment;
- Those not found written in the book of life will have their part in the lake of fire. Burning fire destroys sin and saves man;
- There is a future life for all men in righteousness after judgment;
- Believers will be heirs of God and joint-heirs with Jesus Christ in their kingdom, glory and creation;
- God will become "*all in all.*"

We have all gone astray, every way unto ourselves.

Because we bought the "*BIG LIE*" by believing the enemy that we won't surely die but can have immortality apart from God, true repentance is our first step to a change of heart. We are encouraged to repent for not trusting and believing God, for the deception we have accepted in our lives, and for despising wisdom and instruction.

> *I tell you, Nay: but,* **except ye repent, ye shall** *all likewise* **perish.** *(Luke 13:3, 5)*

> *As many as I love, I rebuke and chasten:* **be zealous** *[desire]* **therefore, and repent.** *(Revelation 3:19)*

> *Likewise, I say unto you, there is* **joy in the presence of the angels of God over one sinner that repenteth.** *(Luke 15:10)*

Sincerely believing something with all our heart doesn't make it true.

Often we can be heard saying: "*Well, God knows my heart*" to justify our behavior based on how we feel instead of what God has said. God indeed knows our heart; it's deceitful above all things and desperately wicked. We can't even know our hearts so believing something with all our heart doesn't necessarily make it true.

> *There is a way that seemeth right unto a man, but the end thereof are the ways of death*. *(Proverbs 14:12, 16:25)*

> *Every way of a man is right in his own eyes: but the LORD pondereth the hearts. (Proverbs 21:2)*

> *The **heart is deceitful above all things** ... (Jeremiah 17:9)*

> *For **as he thinketh in his heart, so is he** ... (Proverbs 23:7)*

We are encouraged to study and let the Spirit teach us about all things.

> *But the Comforter, which is the Holy Ghost, whom the Father will send in my name, **he shall teach you all things**, and bring all things to your remembrance, whatsoever I have said unto you. (John 14:26)*

> *But the anointing which ye have received of him abideth in you, and **ye need not that any man teach you**: but as **the same anointing teacheth you of all things, and is truth, and is no lie**, and even as it hath taught you, ye shall abide in him. (1 John 2:27)*

> *[5] **Trust in the LORD** with all thine heart; and **lean not unto thine own understanding**. [6] In all thy ways acknowledge him, and **he shall direct thy paths**. (Proverbs 3:5-6)*

What to choose?

Will we now go forth with our newly discovered knowledge or will we despise Scripture because it doesn't fit our current beliefs? Will we plant our feet and hold fast to defend our favorite, false doctrines? The decision is rightly called "our choice."

The fear [reverence] of the LORD is the beginning of knowledge: but **fools despise wisdom and instruction.** *(Proverbs 1:7)*

[14] Now therefore fear the LORD, and **serve him in sincerity and in truth** ... *[15] And* **if it seem evil unto you to serve the LORD, choose you this day whom ye will serve ... but as for me and my house, we will serve the LORD.** *(Joshua 24:14-15)*

Truth doesn't change; we only change what we know.

Thank you for walking this journey with me.

The LORD bless thee, and keep thee:
The LORD make his face shine upon thee, and be gracious unto thee:
The LORD lift up his countenance upon thee, and give thee peace.

(Numbers 6:24-26)

Acknowledgment

It would be impossible to acknowledge everyone who has been an essential part of this book. You are the "unsung hero" who has contributed so generously to the outcome but receives no outward recognition for your efforts.

I am truly grateful for your help.

- You gave me encouragement;
- You gave me suggestions;
- You gave me correction;
- You gave me freely of your time;
- You gave me disagreement;
- You gave me so much more.

Everything you gave me only strengthened my resolve to dig deeper for God's treasures.

Although you are not acknowledged here by name, God knows who you are and what you have so generously given. Your reward will be from Him and far greater than your name on this page. This page is fleeting; He is not.

> "… *remember the words of the Lord Jesus, how he said,*
> **It is more blessed to give than to receive**. *(Acts 20:35)*

THANK YOU!

Recommended Links and Further Reading

Links.

www.whathappenswhenwedie.org
  For further study.

www.revelationtimelinedecoded.com
  The best I have ever seen together in one place, Revelation prophecy decoded.

www.graceevangel.org
  Author: *At the End of the Ages, The Abolition of Hell* – Bob Evely

www.goodnewsaboutGod.com
  Author: *Who Rewrote the Bible* – Dr. Lorraine Day

http://www.jglm.org/
  John G. Lake Ministries – Curry Blake

www.sheldonemrylibrary.com/welcome.htm
  Pastor Sheldon Emry (1926-1985)

http://www.e-sword.net/
  The Sword of the Lord with an electronic edge.

www.cgom.org
> Church of God Outreach Ministries: *"Where Are Enoch & Elijah?"*

Your comments.

I welcome your comments. Show me an error and I will correct it. You can email them to me at: bledford7711@gmail.com

For additional copies of this book.

You can order additional hard copies and eBooks on Amazon.com.